WE ARE ONE VOICE

Edited By

SIMON S. MAIMELA
and
DWIGHT N. HOPKINS

WIPF & STOCK · Eugene, Oregon

Wipf and Stock Publishers
199 W 8th Ave, Suite 3
Eugene, OR 97401

We Are One Voice
Black Theology in the USA and South Africa
By Maimela, Simon S. and Hopkins, Dwight N.
Copyright©1989 by Maimela, Simon S.
ISBN 13: 978-1-5326-1943-4
Publication date 3/24/2017
Previously published by Skotaville Publishers, 1989

Table of Contents

    Editors   (v)
    Contributors   (vii)
    Introduction   (ix)

1. Survival and Liberation in Black Faith   1

2. The Socio-Cultural Analysis of the Origins and Development of Black Theology   35

3. Black Feminist Theology in South Africa   51

4. The Emergence of a Black Feminist Theology in the United States   61

5. Present Socio-Political - Economic Movements for Change - U S Perspective   73

6. Present Socio-Political - Economic Movements for change - S A Perspective   87

7. Theological Reflection on Black Theology   97

8. Black Theological Perspectives - Past and Present   105

9. The Future and Mutual Support - *Zama Asefani*   127

10. Prospects for the Future and Building of Alliances   139

    Epilogue and Prospect   151

EDITORS

Simon S Maimela received his Ph.D degree from Harvard University, and is Professor of Systematic Theology at the University of South Africa in Pretoria.

Dwight N Hopkins was awarded a Ph.D degree by Union Theological Seminary, New York, and is Assistant Professor of Religious and Ethnic Studies at Santa Clara University in California.

CONTRIBUTORS

Kelly D Brown, a minister of the Episcopal Church, is presently teaching systematic theology at Howard University Divinity School in Washington, DC

James Cone, a minister of the African Methodist Episcopal Church, is Charles A Briggs, Distinguished Professor of Systematic Theology at Union Theological Seminary, New York.

Roxanne Jordan, is pastor of the Jeffrey's Bay Congregational Church, Cape Province, South Africa.

Simon Maimela, a minister of the Evangelical Lutheran Church, is Professor of Systematic Theology at the University of South Africa, Pretoria.

Takatso Mofokeng, a minister of the (black) Dutch Reformed Church, teaches systematic theology at the University of South Africa, Pretoria.

Itumeleng Mosala, a Methodist minister, teaches Old Testament and Black Theology at the University of Cape Town.

Cecil Ngcokovane, a Presbyterian minister, teaches Social Ethics at the Federal Theological Seminary, Natal Province, South Africa.

Gayraud S Wilmore is Professor of Afro-American Studies at New York Theological Seminary, New York.

Cornel West, is currently Director of Afro-American Studies and Professor in the Religious Department at Princeton University.

Josiah Young, a Methodist minister, is assistant professor of systematic theology at Wesley Theological Seminary in Washington, DC

Introduction

Dwight N. Hopkins

December 1 – 3, 1986 marked a major milestone in the development of black theology. For the first time ever since the start of contemporary black theology (1966), black theologians from the United States and South Africa formally assembled to share and explore a common black theological agenda. This conference successfully inaugurated the initial organizing process of dialogue on God's liberating activity among black North Americans and black South Africans. In the papers presented, brothers and sisters of the African diaspora reaffirmed a distinct thrust, that of the black poor. Thus those in attendance continued to elaborate on the progressive and transformative emphasis in black theology. In addition to reaffirmation of God's chosen people (i.e., 'the least of these'), representatives from both continents showed how diverse black theological voices continue to unite against the brutal assaults of white theology. But presenters moved well beyond a mere anti-white posture. Indeed until this gathering on the eve of the 21st century, nowhere had there been such a relatively comprehensive notation of common theological agenda items, spanning black biblical hermeneutics, the theological significance of black working class culture, to the contributions of women in black theology. In a sense, the conference coalesced in one setting the multifaceted concerns of black theology in the last two decades. Hence these papers underscore a coming together of ongoing theological discussions taking place in the USA and South Africa. At the same time, they serve as indicators of future foundational issues. And in fact, it is this characteristic of the conference - both its benchmarking of essential points and charting the outlines of future discourse - that greatly stamps its uniqueness. For, never in recent times have black religious colleagues from North America and South Africa joined hands in a united effort to say who they are and where they wish to be.

Held at Union Theological Seminary in New York and sponsored by the Ecumenical Association of Third World Theologians (EATWOT), the Institute for Contextual Theology (South Africa), and Union Seminary's Ecumenical Program and Theological Field, the gathering offered theologians a face-to-face engagement over their common histories and theological themes. This book represents the papers presented at this three day conference.

First, a word on the idea for the conference. During the summer of 1985, professors James Cone and Cornel West journeyed to South Africa and there met several black theologians, professors Simon Maimela, Bonganjalo Goba, Takatso Mofokeng and others. In conversation, they discovered the need to share in dialogue and exchange around the origin and common concerns of black theology in both contexts. True, individual black theologians from both countries had read each others' writings and had met individually in diverse dialogical settings. But in the twenty year history of contemporary black theology (1966-1986), never had they assembled as black religious thinkers for the sole purpose of examining their common unities and disunities.

Similarities and Differences

Sharing a parallel historical origin, both black theologies sprang from a similar resistance to white supremacy's attempt to crush black reality into a subservient invisibility. Against such attacks, black theology in the United States and South Africa fought back by correctly claiming God's creation and affirmation of blackness. Even further, black religious thinkers on both sides of the Atlantic called Euro-North American theology to task for the latter's *heretical* failure. In particular, the dominant white theology had not placed liberation of the poor at the centre of the gospel message. Over against white theology's assertion of its normalcy, black theologians proudly renamed themselves as God's children and vehemently denounced white religious thought as the work of the Anti-Christ.

Black theology in the USA and South Africa share similarities and differences. North American black theology arose in response to the Civil Rights and Black Power movements of the 1960s. Symbolized by Martin Luther King, Jr., the Civil Rights movement linked the gospel message directly to the freedom of black Americans. Thus King and his followers called into question the prevailing status-quo white theology. Black power, the other major influence on black theology, grew in reaction to white liberal hypocrisy and the intransigence of white American racism (i.e., most signified by the brutal assassination of America's foremost prophet of non-violence, Martin King). The post-King era, then, marked black America's turn toward the trenchant critique of Malcolm X (e.g., a philosophy of self-determination and by-any-means-necessary for black people). In a word, black theology in the USA originated to synthesize Malcolm X's black liberation and Martin King's integration approaches.[1]

Like black theology in North America, black theology in South Africa grew in response to white racism (e.g., liberal and conservative) and the Black Consciousness Movement. From the early 1960s to 1968, white liberal organizations provided the only legal national forum in which blacks could politically meet. However black South Africans found that though liberal whites professed 'multiracialism', they adhered to apartheid's segregation laws and, thus, enjoyed white privileges. Consequently beginning in 1968, Steve Biko led a nationwide movement for black solidarity and black self-determination. With black consciousness, black pastors and black theologians looked to a 'fighting God'. They prayed to a God who affirmed the beauty of blackness and the ability of the black community to do for itself without reliance on white leadership and participation. In brief, black South Africans discovered that the Black Messiah of their pan-African sisters and brothers in North America was the same God liberating the poor in their own land.[2]

However, a similar historical origin and common theological themes should not obscure the distinct conditions of black theology on the African and North American continents. Specifically, black Americans suffer the experience of an oppressed minority engulfed by the white supremacy of a majority population. In contrast, black South Africans, given their overwhelming population, exhibit the potential to one day overrun their minute white apartheid clique. Futhermore, black Americans continually undergo the tug between their Americanness and the nagging question mark about their African heritage pre-slavery (what WEB DuBois called 'this double-consciousness').[3] Quite the opposite, black South Africans have a direct connection to their land, indigenous language, African culture, and African traditional religions. Evenmore, black Americans have currently ruled out organized violent resistance to racism. Taking an opposite approach, black South Africans have integrated self-defensive violence within their liberation struggle. Finally, black Americans have not articulated a clear radical critique of society. Black South African opposition groups, on the other hand, are generally intentionally anti-capitalist and much more open to socialist ideas.

Conference Papers

It was precisely their similarities, and divergences, over a theological interpretation of God's liberation of the oppressed black experience that drew black theologians together at the December 1986 conference. Indeed, the conference structure sought to lend a full exploration and hearing of such unities and disunities. For example, a representative from each country was assigned to offer views on one of the five theological topics. Thus ten persons presented papers all together.

The conference began with the first session's theme: *'Historical, Social and Cultural Origins of Black Theology'*. From the USA side, we include a contribution from Gayraud S Wilmore.[4] His essay, *'Survival and Liberation in Black Faith,'* places black religious thought within its historical perspective. Rooting this thought in the experience of transplanted Africans in North America slavery, Wilmore asserts that religion has been the principal mode of expression of African-Americans' 'peoplehood'. Continuing, Wilmore establishes the themes of survival and liberation as foundational in black religion. To discover black religious thought, he directs our eyes down to black 'folk', where we encounter their religio-cultural consciousness of God. Thus one of Wilmore's contributions in his measuring the depths of the black folk sacred cosmos which, according to him, is not only churchly and religious, but also extra-church (e.g. in the pool halls and on the street corners of black North America). Finally with his three-part definition of sources required for the doing of black theology, Wilmore contributes directly to the dialogue between black religious scholars in North America and South Africa.

Focusing on the origin and development of South African black theology, Cecil Ngcokovane acknowledges the importance of the definitional stage. Yet at the same time, he admonishes his black South African colleagues for their laxity in the actual construction phase, that is, the actual doing of black theology in South Africa. Therefore, he calls for a turn to and deepening of content, methodology, and conceptual tools of analysis. Emphasizing the centrality of black labor in a constructive black theology, Ngcokovane's views signify the growing influence of historical materialist and political economic analyses among South African black religious thinkers.

Following this discussion on the historical origins, the conference then proceeded to session two: 'Black Feminist Theology'. Here a persistent and recurring theme throughout the gathering jelled with the papers by Roxanne Jordan and Kelly D. Brown. Brown offers a broad sweep of the progress of a North American black feminist theology. Furthermore, she delineates the nuanced directions this theology is assuming. Likewise, Jordan expresses the pain of black South African women as they struggle with their men in the liberation movement against apartheid. From the particular experiences of black women in both contexts, a unique black women's perspective on the Christian faith emerges. Indeed, the challenge to black theology, exemplified by Brown and Jordan, is exactly the call for recognition and incorporation of the specifically unique relation of black women to the gospel message of liberation. For example, black women shoulder a disproportionate burden within the liberation movement and within the black church. Yet their voices are silenced and their leadership potential is stifled by black male 'comrades', preachers, and theologians. Nonetheless, black women remain undaunted. The pervasiveness of their critique and the slow, but growing, response of black men is witnessed in nearly all the conference papers. Brown and Jordan have elevated the authenticity of black theological discourse. Hence, one cannot remain a true Christian without acknowledging, prioritizing, and fighting for the freedom of black women.

The third session of the conference fell within the area of 'Present Socio-Political-Economic Movements for Change'. Here Cornel West's paper pursues a three part approach in answering the question: what does it take to be a Christian in situations of intense race, gender, and class oppression? West responds at three levels - the normative, social analysis, and praxis. But it is on the second level, social analysis, that he unravels the complexities and multi-layered reality of black oppression. West weaves together various social evils of exploitation (i.e., capitalist economics), domination (i.e., bureaucracies), repression (i.e., violence of the state), and subjugation (i.e., racism and sexism). Drawing on Marx, Weber, Foucaux, and Garvey (as well as Malcolm X), West continues to press black theology to take seriously the theoretical and practical import of prophetic analytical tools.[5]

Complementing West, Simon Maimela's paper takes us through the various movements for change within present-day South Africa. Maimela astutely uncovers the maneuvering on the part of the apartheid government, white capitalist private interests, and white attempts at 'dialogue' with the oppressed black majority. He ends his views with an account of the 'people's resistance' for change. Emphasizing the cutting edge position of the Kairos theologians, he highlights the progressive role that the black church can play in defeating apartheid and reconstructing a new South Africa. Despite the desperate attempts of the racist government to maintain their rule (magnified by continued states of emergencies), Maimela's paper clearly indicates the heightening realignment of all class forces in response to the persistent struggle of black South Africa.[6]

In the fourth session of the conference, *'Theological Reflection'*, James Cone frames and capsulizes major issues for a focused inter-continental discussion. He touches on five areas facing the conference and black theology as a whole. Cone begins with the oppressed status of women within the black theological dialogue. As the father of contemporary black theology, his accent on black feminist theology seeks to add weight to the prioritization of the specificity of black women's contributions to the black church and the black community. Next he tackles the issues of 'race and class' and 'scripture's authority'. Cone draws lessons from the debilitating effect of pitting race and class analyses. This advice he shares with his South African colleagues who currently are experiencing the dilemma of resolving the inter-connectedness of race and class. Continuing, Cone comments on the increased challenge to scripture's authority in black theological discourse. He notes the profound ambiguity of the bible and calls for further discussion. Finally, he urges the broadening of black theology into two directions. More specifically, he urges further linking black theology with the international arena; a global connection with the poor, particularly in the third world. And Cone presses black theology to move from the seminaries to the churches.

Takatso Mofokeng's 'theological reflection' paper calls on black theology in South Africa to develop another theological language. The present apartheid state of emergency, in his opinion, necessitate more concentration on black theological methodology. Thus Mofokeng pinpoints an even closer connection between black theology and Black Consciousness.[7] Such a marriage, then, would guard against white liberal influences in black discourse. Further deepening theology in black consciousness concerns, Mofokeng opts for a strict reliance on black sources in the doing of theology. For him, black culture, history, and African Traditional religions reign supreme. Accordingly, he signals a pan-African relation between black theology on both sides of the Atlantic.

The fifth and final aspect of the conference, 'the *Future and Mutual Support*', heard papers from Josiah Young and Itumeleng Mosala. Young, echoing Mofokeng, pursues a distinctly pan-African black theology. In fact, drawing on the historical relation between both countries, Young depicts white supremacy as bonding North American blacks closer to South Africans than to the rest of the African continent. Expounding his unique contribution of a pan-African black theology, Young visions a mutual relation built on love, commitment, and solidarity.[8]

Mosala's presentation sees the need for a 'projective task', that is, a description of the new society for which black theology struggles. Without a radical projection in the interests of the poor, black theology's and the black church's new society in North America and South Africa stands victim to white liberal subterfuge. Indeed, Mosala contends, South African white 'progressives' have already redefined black theology and silenced it in favor of Latin American Liberation Theology. In addition, Mosala boldly hints at a moratorium on other aspects of black theological discussion in favor of a singular focus on black women's concern. Though no one has replied to his implied proposal, nonetheless his emphasis represents the extent of black women's influence in South African theology. Finally, Mosala argues for employing a radical social analysis in the establishment of a new biblical hermeneutic. In brief, he discovers two 'gods' in the bible; a god of the ruling class oppressor and the God of poor black working class culture. Only by sifting out the liberating God will black theology shake off its methodological and epistemological dependence on white hermeneutical privilege.[9]

The papers in this volume hail the diversity and vibrancy of black theology in the USA and South Africa. Drawn together around the gospel mandate to reclaim God's creation of black humanity and to fight white supremacy, both theologies display a growing maturity in relating the complex evils of race, gender, and class (i.e., both domestic capitalism and international imperialism). As reflected in this book, the dialogue is only in its beginning stages; exploring and sharing each others' contexts, defining common issues, isolating main agenda concerns, and gropingly mapping future relations. However, we should not miss the crucial importance of this first conference. It portends the struggle of the black poor to come to terms with their religious, political, and cultural identity independent of the established white religious channels of seminary and missionary. Moreover, it suggests the black community's right to think theologically and to organize internationally. For certainly, the unity of black theology USA and black theology South Africa intimates a strengthening of the movement of the world's poor - those for whom Jesus died and was resurrected - against United States imperialism and apartheid South Africa - two of the greatest purveyors of white supremacy in the history of humankind. And in this pan-African black theological discourse, we also see a grappling for the seeds of a new future; an earthly, penultimate future in which the poor, the world's majority, communally own and distribute all of God's resources to all of God's creation regardless of color or gender. Indeed, only in such new social relations can the black poor realize their full cultural, political, and spiritual emancipation.

FOOTNOTES

1. For more on the rise Black Theology in the USA see James Cone's *For My People: Black Theology and the Black Church* (Maryknoll, N.Y.: Orbis Books, 1984) Chapter 1; his *Speaking The Truth: Ecumenism, Liberation, and Black Theology* (Grand Rapids, Michigan: Eerdmans Publishing Co., 1986) pp.83-111; Gayraud Wilmore's *Black Religion and Black Radicalism: An interpretation of the Religious History of Afro-American People,* 2nd edition (Maryknoll, N.Y.: Orbis Books, 1983); and Dwight N Hopkins' 'Black Theology in USA & South Africa: Political and Cultural Liberation,' (Ph.D. dissertation, Union Theological Seminary, New York, 1988,) Chapter one.
2. For more about black consciousness, see Steve Biko I write What I like, ed. Aelred Stubbs (San Francisco: Harper and Row, 1986): Ranwedzi Nengwenkulu, 'The Meaning of Black Consciousness in the Struggle for liberation in South Africa,' in United Nations Centre Against Apartheid, *Notes and Documents,* 16/76 (New York: United Nations, July 1976); and Hopkins, op.cit., chapter one. On the origin of black theology in South Africa, see Basil Moore, ed. *The Challenge of Black Theology in South Africa* (Atlanta: John Knox Press, 1974); and Hopkins, ibid.
3. W E B Du Bois, *The Souls of Black Folk* (New York: The New American Library, 1969), p.45.
4. The actual USA presentor on this topic was Dr. James M Washington (Union Theological Seminary, New York City). However, for this book, we include an edited version of Wilmore's chapter nine in his *Black Religion and Black Radicalism* (Maryknoll, New York: Orbis Books, 1983).
5. See Cornel West, *Prophesy Deliverance; an Afro-American revolutionary christianity* (Philadelphia, Penn.: Westminister Press, 1982)

6. For a fuller account of Maimela's theological views, see his *Proclaim Freedom To My People* (Johannesburg, South Africa: Skotaville Publishers, 1987).
7. On the impact of Black Consciousness in Mofokeng's position, see his *The Crucified Among the Crossbearers: Towards a Black Christology* (Kampen, Netherlands: J H Kok, 1983.
8. Josiah Young, *Black And African Theologies: Siblings or Distant Cousins?* (Maryknoll, N.Y.: Orbis Books, 1986).
9. See Mosala's *Biblical Hermeneutics and Black Theology In South Africa* (Grand Rapids, Mich.: Eerdmans, forthcoming).

1

Survival and Liberation in Black Faith

Gayraud S. Wilmore

> *This is the gift of the Black Folk to the new world. Thus in singular and fine sense the slave became master, the bond servant became free and the meek not only inherited the earth but made their heritage a thing of questing for eternal youth, of fruitful labor, of joy and music, of the free spirit and of the ministering hand, of wide and poignant sympathy with men in their struggle to live and love which is, after all, the end of striving.*
>
> W.E.B. Du Bois,
> *The Gift of Black Folk*

The two assertions of this book are (1) that within American culture as a whole there has been and continues to be an exceedingly complex and distinctive subculture that may be designated black or Afro-American, and (2) that legislation has been and continues to be an essential thread in the fabric of black culture despite black sociological heterogeneity with respect to such secular factors as regional differences and socio-economic backgrounds.

Religiousness, oscillating between conservatism and racialism, has been an enduring characteristic of black life not only in the United States but also in Africa and the Carribean. Religious institutions, therefore, are of the greatest importance in these societies. To them accrues the primary responsibility for the conversation, enhancement, and further development of that distinctive spiritual quality that has enabled blacks to survive and flourish

under some unfavourable conditions of the modern world.
The Afro-American Experience

I have focused attention primarily upon the Afro-American experience. From the earliest days of their captivity in the New World, the transplanted Africans, denied access to other forms of self-affirmation and group power, have used religion and religious institutions as the principal expression of their peoplehood and their will both to exist and to improve their situation. Black religion, fluctuating between protest and accomodation, and protesting in the context of accomodating strategies, has contributed considerably to the ability of Afro-Americans to survive the worst forms of dehumanisation and oppression. Beyond survival, as leaders and followers became more sophisticated about how to use religion, it has helped them to free themselves, first from slavery, then from civil inequality and subordination, to go on to greater heights of personal and group achievement.

Black religion has not always in all circumstances functioned for the advancement of blacks and the solution of some of their most perplexing problems. But it is difficult to understand how even the most skeptical observers of the black religious experience in America can deny that on the whole religion and religious have served blacks well. One can scarcely imagine how they would have fared without them.

In a sense not true of any other immigrant group that came to America, the irreducible problem of the Africans who were brought to this country was survival. For two hundred years slavery in Protestant North America, unlike in the Carribean and Latin America, was practically devoid of mitigating influences from the side of either church or state. Blacks, scattered in small, relatively isolated groups, were reduced to the level of beasts of burden. With but few exceptions they were treated as slightly more than mere animals who were fed, clothed, and sheltered to no greater degree than was necessary to protect the original investment made to procure them. Owners exacted from such property the maximum amount of gainful work their bodies would bear.

The argument that slavery in the South was mainly a paternalistic institution should not be permitted to disguise the fact that blacks reciprocated to the blandishments of their supposedly conscience-stricken masters in their own way, and that force and violence were required to establish and maintain the system. Genovese, a Major prophet of the paternalism thesis, acknowledges that it must not be interpreted as evidence of how slavery was for most blacks or how readily they acquiesced in it:

> The slaves accepted the doctrine of reciprocity, but with a profound difference. To the idea of reciprocal duties they added their own doctrine of reciprocal rights. To the tendency to make them creatures of another's will they counterposed a tendency to assert themselves as autonomous human beings. And that thereby contributed, as they had to, to the generation of conflict and great violence.[1]

Paternalism, in fact, never really worked as it was supposed to. Slave holders were obliged, sooner or later, to recognize that there was extreme insecurity in their situation. Only the most stupid could have mistaken the fact that they were not dealing with black 'sons and daughters' who loved them as a seignorial fathers and exchanged that love for protection, but with thinking, sensible human beings who could never be trusted, precisely on that account, to respond in the same manner as children. Moreover, whatever feelings of warmth or tenderness may have been engendered in day-to-day relationships they would necessarily have to be subordinated to the hard, cold fact that the bottom line was economic value. In the final analysis that value was realistically considered and made secure by the imposition of discipline and the monopoly of violent power that legally and otherwise remained in the hands of the master.

Can anyone imagine that the slave did not know that the *noblesse oblige* of a fawning Christian master depended mainly upon the slave's capability of producing wealth in the same sense that it was produced by the master's mule or cotton gin, a wealth to which the slave had no rightful claim? Against this reduction to the status of a thing, a status enforced by unpredictable cruelty and ruthlessness, the slave's basic obsession was somehow 'to make it,' to hold body and soul together for as long as possible, to engage in an unceasing interior struggle to preserve physical existence and mental sanity — in short, to survive. Survival, therefore, became the regulative principle of the slave community, particularly among field hands, and this single factor best explains the tenacity and functionality of black religion in the plantation South.

As a result of new research during the past several years, we now have a somewhat better idea than previously of how this happened.[2] Drawn together in the quarters after sundown and on Sundays and holidays, the slaves pieced together the tattered remnants of their African past and new patterns of response to the American environment. They selectively chose for themselves attitudes of disbelief, codes dissimulation and subterfuge, structures of meaning — in short, a view of reality and coping skills that made human survival possible under the conditions of their enslavement.

In the formation of a new common language, in the telling of animal tales and proverbs, in the leisure-time practice of remembered handicrafts, in the preparation of foods, homemade medicines, and magical potions and charms, in the standardization of rituals of birth, marriage, and death, in the creation of modes of play and parody, in the expression of favorite style of singing, instrumental music, and the dance — in all this and by these and other means — the slaves wove for themselves the tapestry of a new African-American culture. It was a culture of human survival in the face of legal oppression and forcible acculturation. It was a culture impregnated with spiritual and occult elements of African, European, and American origin, integrated around a basically religious conception of life and reality.

From the beginning certain men and women who possessed power for both good and evil, a talent for sorcery and divination, exercised extraordinary influence over the slaves. In some slave narratives and reports of white missionaries, they occassionally appear as the first recognized leaders of the community, respected and feared by both slaves and the masters. It was through these specialists in magic, conjuration, and the healing arts that what was left of the old African traditional religions was transplanted and re-intergrated into the new culture of the slaves.[3] To the misery and hopelessness of the slave quarters these specialists brought the consolation and sense of the possibility of transcending external circumstances that helped to make physical and mental survival achievable. The invocation of mystical powers counteracted some of the magic of whites and the wretchedness of daily life. It gave a dimension of depth and ultimacy to the struggle for survival. At that deeper level the reinterpretation and synthesis of transplanted and newly acquired religious systems, mainly evangelical Protestantism, produced a new religious consciousness.

It was out of this mystical, survival-oriented religious consciousness, part African and part European, that they shout songs and spirituals emerged on the plantations, expressing the loneliness and sorrow of a stolen people, but at the same time celebrating the sheer fact of survival despite the contant experience of brutality in the fields, and death and disease in the living quarters. The awakening of white evangelical Christianity in the South during the second quarter of the eighteenth century made contact with this affirmative side of slave religion. Gradually a white-controlled black church evolved from the secret, shaman-led religious meetings in the cabins and brush arbors. But the white preachers and missionaries could never be sure what kind of religion their sermons and camp meetings were crafting.

Christianity did not sweep through the slave community at anything like the rate that some earlier scholars assumed.[4] The Society for the Propagation of the Gospel reported only 40 adult baptisms and 179 baptized children after some eight years of SPG labor among the relatively large slave population of New York City in the early 1700s. It is estimated that in 1750 there were only a thousand baptised slaves in Virginia — about 1 percent of the black population of the colony.

It must also be taken into account that even those slaves who accepted white preaching and made a profession of faith exasperated their mentors by the way they apparently drifted in and out of the state of grace, clinging to dreams, beliefs in ghosts, good-luck charms, and the efficacy of the hoodoo man or the root doctor. Some missionaries and travelers simply branded black religion as insincerity or superstition far distant from anything that could be called Christianity. The slaves were *surviving*, not being smitten with the cogency of Puritan theology.

If whites thought that they were dealing with children who could not discern the difference between white theology and white behavior they were sadly mistaken. As John Lovell, Jr., has observed, 'The slave relied upon religion, not primarily because he felt himself 'converted'; but because he recognized the power inherent in religious things.'[5] That power had to do, first of all, with the necessity, of survival — with the creation of an alternative reality system that could keep the slave alive and possessed of some modicum of sanity. The protest and resistance elements we find in early forms of black folk religion in the Carribean and in the south-eastern United States express the determination to survive against all odds.

We should not be surprised to find, therefore, a dark and contrary side of black religion as it developed under the most trying circumstances. In Haiti it is in the difference between the Arada and the Petro rites of vodun that we see the separation of a religion of survival from one with more possibilities for refinement in the direction of sociability and edification. The same thing can be said about the difference between the religion of the black Methodists in Charleston and that of other black Methodists in Philadelphia during the first quarter of the nineteenth century, when, incidentally, the example of Haiti was most vivid in the minds and imagination of blacks throughout the United States.

The dark and contrary side of black religion must be understood as an alternative form of spirituality. It is a fundamental aspect of what we may call the survival tradition. It has been imprinted on a persistently heterodox form of Christianity that has come down through black churches and cults into this century. Although it was often expressed as a curiously divergent form of black spirituality, it is not to be equated with the kind of pietism that can be translated into social reform. It often had, rather, a bitter unsentimentality about it. It was more often cynical, manipulative and, at the very least, ambivalent about spiritual things. Horace Cayton and St. Clair Drake found it in the Chicago ghetto during the Depression of the 1930s.[6] It is not surprising, therefore, that C. Eric Lincoln observed the same spirit, in contrast to orthodox Islam, in the bitterness and hatred of the early Black Muslim movement.[7]

This bitter realism and irony that comes strangely mixed with religiosity antedated the great migration. There were the 'upstart crows' in the Southland. Churchgoers circulated songs and sayings irreverent of traditional religion:

> *Our father, who art in heaven*
> *White man owe me 'leven and pay me seven.*
> *Thy kingdom come, thy will be done,*
> *If I hadn't tuck that, I wouldn't got none.*[8]

There was a sense of the ironic and tragic in the slave secular songs and early blues. A sense that there is something out there in inexorable opposition to one's most ardent aspirations and pretensions. But if we are too 'upity' and remember that we are all, whether black or white, poor creatures bound to die, it is possible to 'overcome someday.' Other powers are available to help us to survive.

W.E.B. Du Bois was the first to recognize this extraordinary aspect of black folk religion. He speaks of 'the peculiar ethical paradox' facing black life at the turn of the century that was transforming black Christianity. It was the paradox of the impotence, bitterness, and vindictiveness of migrants who still believe in God, but those whose 'religion, instead of worship, is a complaint and a curse, a wail rather than a hope, a sneer rather than a faith' as they faced the poverty and despair of the Northern ghetto.[9] The other side of the paradox was what he called the shrewd 'Jesuitic casuistry' of the black farmhand who remained in the post-Reconstruction South, forced to take advantage of the inherent weakness of the white man's position by deception and hypocrisy, and willing, if necessary, to play the role of Uncle Tom, stooping in order to conquer.[10]

These two divergent tendencies in black ethics and religious life — the first tending toward radicalism, the other toward hypocritical compromise — represent two strands of a survival tradition. These strands of religion belong to what Lawrence W. Levine differentiated from traditional Christianity and called the slaves' 'instruments of life, of sanity, of health, and of selfrespect.'[11]

Du Bois had an unfailing insight into the true situation. He recognized that what the white evangelical churches had passed on to blacks had been thoroughly adulterated by the end of slavery, merged with a subterranean stream of African spirituality and the survival instincts of an impoverished and downtrodden people. In this condition, he wrote, 'broods silently the deep religious feeling of the real Negro heart, the stirring, unguided might of powerful human souls who have lost the guiding star of the past and seek in the great night of a new religious ideal.'[12]

Perhaps it would be more accurate simply to speak of this form of black religion as a tendency or a tradition rather than an ideal toward which black believers strove. In any case, it was persistent quality of the folk tradition that should disabuse us of the much too facile assumption of some scholars that black religion was nothing more than an echo of nineteenth-century revivalism, a little louder and more emotional. It had primarily to do with survival rather than liberation, although there is a complex relationship between the more aggressive form of survivalism and the left wing of the liberation tradition of the establishment black denominations. But the survival tradition was more characteristic of 'the invisible institution' and gave the white missionaries much difficulty. Through storefront religion and black pentecostalism it laid the foundation for the paradoxical culture that Du Bois saw invading the black urban community at the turn of the century.

Du Bois spoke of survival religion as the search for a 'new religious ideal,' breaking with the conventional pietism and fundamentalism of the Southern Methodist and Baptist churches that attempted to shape black religiosity between 1830 and the beginning of the Civil War. But whether powered by a new ideal or whether it was simply an instinctive recoil from white religion, the survival form was never completely domesticated by evangelicalism. It preserved an alternative tradition in the black subculture that has reserved (to use Paul Lehmann's felicitous phrase) 'to make and to keep life human.'

Daniel Alexander Payne, the great patriarch of the African Methodist Episcopal Church, fought against lower-class, survival-oriented folk religion throughout his long ministry. The passion with which he attempted to drive it out of the AME church is proof of its tenacity even in that bastion of black Christian respectability. Bishop Payne was not mistaken in his assumption that what he was witnessing was not conversion to the religion of John Wesley or fidelity to the discipline of Asbury and Allen, but something very different and possibly heretical. He encountered a mysterious form of virtue, in the sense of the Latin *virtus*, or the term 'manna' as used by anthropologists — a power or force of casual efficacy and creative vitality — something of which it is of the greatest advantage for one to possess. It was what West African priests would have recognized as both proceeding from and capable of influencing the gods and the ancestors. It was a power that could be used to ward off evil, to perform good, and to keep body and soul together against every destructive element of the universe — in other words, the power to be, the power to survive.

Leonard E. Barrett writes that this form of religion asserted itself, to the consternation of missionaries, in the great Jamaican revival of 1860-61.[13] It emerged in several places in the United States in the twentieth century: in the Azusa Streer revival of 1905 in Los Angeles, when Charles Fox Parham and his white followers split with Seymour's black Pentecostals because of 'heathen' manifestations; in the Universal Negro Improvement Association of Marcus Garvey, when West Indian survival religion sought an unusual synthesis with Anglo-Catholicism and Pan-Africanism within the African Orthodox church; in the movement of the Cape Verdian prophet Daddy Grace, who, from a small family church in New Bedford, Massachusetts, built one of the most powerful black religious movements in America.

This survival motif is closely associated with authentic black religion in its alternating phases of withdrawal from and aggressive opposition to the white world. This is what the mysterious Detroit peddlar W.D. Farad combined with a homegrown form of black Muslimism to create the national of Islam. Elijah Muhammad's message attracted so many alienated blacks because they recognized in it accents of a tradition they had known in the rural South where whitenization had been resisted. It is clear that Elijah quoted as frequently from the Bible as from the Koran. His most gifted disciple, Malcolm X, whose father was a Garveyite Baptist preacher, received support from many black Christians who recognized those same accents when Malcolm drew upon a survival form of folk religion to wean the masses away from evangelical Christianity.

The Harlem Renaissance poet Langstone Hughes understood this survival tradition and used it as the basis of some of his best social criticism. He once wrote of those who had been sustained by it:

> But then there are low-down folks, the so-called common element, and they are the majority — may the Lord be praised! The people who have their nip of gin on Saturday nights and are not too important to themselves or the community, or too well fed, or too learned to watch the lazy world go round. They live on 7th Street in Washington, or State Street in Chicago and they do not particularly care whether they are like white folks or anybody else. Their joy runs, bang! into ectasy. Their religion soars to a shout. Work maybe a little today, rest a little tomorrow. Play awhile. Sing awhile. O, let's dance! These common people are not afraid of spirituals, as for a long time their more intellectual brethren were, and jazz is their child. They furnish a wealth of colorful, distinctive material for any artist because they still hold to their own individuality in the face of American standardization.[14]

The connective links between black secular culture and black religion, which were provided by the survival tradition, are explored in much of the literature of black American and the West Indies. They can be found in the poetry of Claude McCay and

Countee Cullen, the novels of Richard Wright and James Baldwin, and the essays of Alice Walker, Andrew Salkey, and Derek Walcott. As ever, creative artists often see more clearly than do theologians the dimensions of life and culture that transcend philosophical speculation and expose the raw and mysterious edges of existence in the language and symbols of the folk mediated through artistic genius.

Survival And Liberation: Two Traditions

Blacks in the United States and the Carribean are, for the most part, Christians. But they are Christians in a way different from what we usually understand by the term. The nonsystematic, ambivalent Christianity of blacks has been understood in terms of evangelicalism and otherworldliness, but it has produced one of the most this-worldly, empirical religious traditions in the New World. Its roots are not in Rome or Geneva, but in Calabar, West Kingston, Jamaica, and the plantation country of North America. We have been deceived into equating it with its subsequent institutionalization in established churches.

Many blacks were converted to white Christianity, but many others were forced, by the sheer dint of irrepressible and what Charles Long calls 'oppugnancy,' to invent a religion of survival. As the Carribean poet Walcott says in an essay on black history, 'What seemed to be surrender was redemption. What seemed the loss of tradition was its renewal. What seemed the death of faith was its rebirth.'[15]

What may be called the liberation tradition in black religion also begins with the determination to survive, but because it is exterior rather than primarily interior (and for that reason its carriers find more space in which to maneuver), it goes beyond strategies of sheer survival to strategies of elevation – from 'make do' to 'must do more.' Both strategies are basic to Afro-American life and culture. They are intertwined in complex ways throughout the history of the diaspora. Both are responses to reality in a dominating white world. Both arise from the same religious sensibility and inheritance that took institutional form in Afro-Christian and Afro-

Islamic cults and sects from the mid-eighteenth century onward.

What Blassingame describes as making the best of a bad situation in the antebellum South is a good example of what we mean by the survival tradition in the literature.

> They simply had to make the best of the situation in which they found themselves. Henry Clay Bruce contended that there were many slaves 'who thought they knew they suffered a great wrong in their enslavement, gave their best services to their masters, realizing, philosophically, that the wisest course was to make the best of their unfortunate situation ...' Frederick Douglass spoke for many of them when he asserted, 'A man's troubles are always half disposed of when he finds endurance his only remedy.' William Grimes indicated the brutal realism and the will to survive of many slaves when he declared that slavery was a cruel institution, 'but being placed in that situation, to repine was useless; we must submit to our fate, and bear up, as well as we can, under the cruel treatment of our despotic tyrants.'[16]

Blacks could not, of course, be expected to concern themselves about liberation unless they first learned how to survive. What we shall call the liberation tradition was grounded in the will to survive, but it went beyond that. It rose above the constraining and pessimistic attitudes of slavery and establishment itself on the higher ground of racial improvement, moral rectitude, and benevolence. William Hamilton, addressing the freemen of the New York African Society in 1809 from the safety of lower Manhattan, could declare:

> The gloomy hermit we pity and the snarling cynic [sic] we despise, these are men who appear to be rubbed off the list of men, they appear to have lost the fine fibres of the mind, on which it depends for expansion and growth, they appear to be sunk into a state of insensibility of the extreme happiness growing out of social life.[17]

In the founding of the Free African Society and other self-help groups of free blacks in several communities we see the original motivation and vitality of the liberation tradition in its early evolution in America. Although the situation of most free blacks was little better than slavery, the effort they made in Charleston with Brown Society, in Boston and Newport with African Unions, and in Philadelphia with the Free African Society demonstrates that their immediate interest was not so much the issue of life and death as mutual encouragement and advancement along the freedom road.

The historic decision that Richard Allen and Absolom Jones made in 1787 to transcend the divisiveness of white denominationalism by organising a nonsectarian society that could solidify the black community for morality, social welfare, and benevolence led directly to the founding of the AME Church and the Episcopal Church of St. Thomas. They were not, of course, so easily to divest themselves of denominationalism, but Allen at least was ultimately successful in wresting control from whites and establishing one of the first national institution concerned about the liberation and uplift of all Afro-Americans.

No example of this motif will serve better to illustrate my point than the independent but church-related American Moral Reform Society, which was created by upper-class blacks at the First African Presbyterian church of Philadelphia in 1837. In their 'Declaration of Sentiment' the founders present a view of the gospel and the responsibility of black Christians that looks in quite another direction from that of the illiterate slave preachers and marginal black Christians of the South:

> We therefore declare to the world, that our object is to extend the principles of universal peace and good will to all mankind, by promoting sound morality, by the influence of education, temperance, economy, and all those virtues that alone can render man acceptable in eyes of God or the civilized world ... Therefore we cheerfully enter on this moral warfare in defence of liberty, justice and humanity, conscious that whether to witness its com-

pletion, or die in anticipation of its glorious results, that it has already been committed to the friends of liberty and Christianity throughout the world.[18]

If it is the slave community of the South where we find the most prominent examples of the survival tradition and can trace it through the slave churches to the heterodox sects and cults of the early twentieth century, it is in the free communities of the North and in Southern cities such as Charleston, Richmond, and New Orleans that we find a developing Christian liberation tradition. It began in the quasi-secular Free African Societies and independent congregations. It continued through the Negro Convention movement, the black press, black abolitionism, the mission to the freedmen, the Niagara Movement, the NAACP, and the National Urban League.

It would be too simplistic to suppose that one tradition was exclusively Southern, rural, and lower-class, whereas the other was exclusively Northern, urban, and aspiring middle-class. Such regional and economic class diferentiations break down at several points. The connection between North and South, slave and free, field hand and house servant, rural peasantry and urban proletariat is too complicated for broad generalization to hold. And yet, with certain qualifications, it is instructive to observe that Afro-American religion, neglected and repressed in the South for more than two centuries, developed a stoical realism and inner strength consistent with its southern environment. On the other hand, in the North, where the church soon found itself catering to a better educated middle class, a different set of norms and values developed. In that setting both radical-aggressive and conservative-avoidance patterns can be indentified, just as among farm workers in the South. But the basic orientation of the liberation was not so much to survive as to liberate by elevating and advancing the American people of African descent in the United States.

Similarly, these two tendencies of Afro-American religion cannot be correlated precisely with the division often made between black separatists and assimilationists. In the controversy among black Baptists over the (white) American Baptist Publication

Society and the development of independent black schools, for example, many ministers in the South, although steeped in the survivalist tradition and the philosophy of Booker T. Washington, opted for friendly co-operation with the Northern white church. On the other hand, liberation-orientated black Presbyterians in the North have shown strong separist tendencies by institutionalizing an ethnic caucus and supporting the black power movement of the 1960s.

All we can say is that there are both separatists and integrationists in the broad spectrum of each tradition. The general direction of survivalist strategies toward an indifference about interracial co-operation while keeping a friendly face, but with a stronger interest in self-help behind the scenes. The general direction of liberationist strategies is toward interracial cooperation, but with a radical disengagement from whites under certain conditions and a willingness to use secular politics rather than church-sponsored bootstrap operations to address the needs of the masses. We may speak of the former as conservative-separist and the latter as progressive-intergrationist, but such labels must be used cautiously and will not hold up in all historical contexts.

Generally speaking, the liberationists black church leaders of the nineteenth century desired to be free from the white control without necessarily rejecting the proffered friendship of whites. Secondly, they sought to promote the moral and cultural advancement of blacks within the American political and economic system. Thirdly, it was their purpose not only to free brothers and sisters in the South by non-violent means, but to champion the cause of the oppressed throughout the world.

The drive for freedom from white control was strongest during the life of Bishop Allen and other preachers who had led their people out of white churches. That characteristic was fairly continuous among the clergy during the nineteenth century, for they wanted desperately to build self-respecting black institutions and believed that it could not be done without cutting the umbilical cord. But after the death of Allen, in 1831, and a secular challenge to the control the preachers exercised over organizations that grew up alongside the black church, there was an increasing deference to white leadership. The close relationship of the liberations with white allies who promised to secure their full civil rights continued to be problematic for the freedom movement outside the black church. Except for periodic disengagements, as when several leading black ministers broke with Garrison in the 1840s and 1850s, it continued up to the founding of the NAACP.

The black church of the middle class illustrates some of the ambiguities of the liberation tradition. Although AME Bishop William Paul Quinn called his denomination a veritable 'anti-slavery society,' and many Northern clergymen were in the forefront of the abolition movement, Frederick Douglass was frequently critical of black churches because they were not as much as they could for the cause of freedom. A strong argument, however, can be that the black churches were the most consistent advocates of the liberation theme throughout the nineteenth century. They were born in a quiet rebellion against white domination. They made the personage and the school house a joint enterprise. For all the energy they gave to building an ecclesiastical structure on a par with white churches, they never forgot those who were still in bondage. What they did not promote officially for black freedom, they promoted unofficially — spinning off secular groups such as the Negro Convention movement. If they seemed unduly cautious about mounting a campaign to arm the slaves and fomenting insurrection, it was because they believed that their primary responsibility was to build an institution that would prepare blacks, morally and spiritually, for that great jubilee that they never doubted would come in God's own time. Moreover, their concern about the redemption of Africa, their participation in Reconstruction politics, their involvement in the founding of scores of colleges and secondly schools in the South, and their struggle for social welfare and civil rights in the North, place the mainline of the black church squarely in the liberation tradition of black religion.

It is important to note, however, that the Southern wing of these churches was often closer to a conservative, a political form of Christianity than to the Christian radicalism of Northerners such as Reverdy Ransome and S.L. Corrothers, both African Methodist leaders, or J. Milton Waldron and Sutton E. Griggs, leaders of the

National Baptists. In any case, it seems clear that the role of the major black denominations in activities one would identify with the liberation streams would contradict the allegation of the distinguished sociologist E. Franklin Frazier that 'the Negro church and Negro religion ... have been responsible for the so-called backwardness of American Negroes.'[19]

When we turn to the smaller denominations founded after the Civil War, most notably those coming out of the Holiness and Pentecostal movements, a somewhat different story emerges.[20] We know, for example, that most of their members were Southern in origin, less educated, and of lower socio-economic status. When they migrated to the North the basic survival orientation of their religion was either continued with a strong rural flavor in an essentially urban milieu, or secularized toward a new alignment of folk religion and racial consciousness.[21]

These smaller denominations deserve much more study than they have received. They represent an important transformation of traditional black religion under urban conditions in the great cities of the North and West. Unlike some of the mainline black churches, they had little interest in racial integration or in achieving the standards of mainline white denominations. They took new form and expression in the ghetto storefront churches that multiplied rapidly in the cities after the First World War. The challenges they presented to the established black churches in communal interaction, in styles of dress and worship, and in their rigid prohibitions against the new fashions and immoralities of the urban ghetto must be understood as a form of judgement against what they regard as dechristianizing influences in mainline black religion as a whole. They were to find, however, a more formidable obstacle to their own brand of religion in the misery and despair of the poor than in competition with the churches of the black bourgeoisie.

It should come as no surprise that we find members of Holiness and Sanctified churches turning up in the Garvey movement, the Moorish Science Tempels of Noble Drew Ali, Father Divine's Peace Mission, and the many nationalist and revitalization cults that emerged during the decades following the First World War. The dechristianization tendency in black culture during this period was partly due to the demoralization of the masses by a poverty and racism that they found more destructive and humiliating in the North than in the South. If new sects and cults were finally able to flourish it was because the survival mechanism that rural blacks found useful in the South for reintepreting white Christianity went through a hardening process that demystified black Christianity in the North and produced a religiously motivated consciousness of color and racial destiny. The black intellectuals and artist of the the Harlem Renaissance period perceived a rich new culture developing out of this urbanization of the survival tradition and their attempt to give it aesthetic meaning and a political voice helped to create a new cultural nationalism in the black communities of the North.

What was happening in this development was the coming together of the survival and liberation motifs of black religion and culture in a new dialectical relationship consonant with the demands of urban existence in a racist society. The black power movement, which emerged from secular activists in the North and the church-based civil rights movements in the South, was the ideological consequence of this convergence. Martin Luther King, Jr., personified the dialectic of the two strands of black religion related to that movement even though he refused to endorse it. Nevertheless, it is in his own development as a national leader that one sees the complex interweaving of a moral sternness fueled by the emotionalism of the mass-based black church of the South and in the social action orientation and universalizing theological liberalism of the Northern seminaries he attended in Chester, Pennysylvania, and Boston, Massachussets. The fact that the Dexter Avenue Baptist church was in Montgomery, Alabama, should not be permitted to confuse the issue. It had a liberationist 'Northern exposure' and stands at one end of King's career; at the other end stands the Mason Temple Church of God in Christ, which he did not pastor, but with which he was involved during the strike of the Memphis garbage workers who were largely members of that survivalist denomination. At the beginning and end, if not throughout his ministry, King wove together these two seminal traditions of black faith.

In one of the most famous sermons King values 'the tough mind ... sharp and penetrating, breaking through the crust of legends and myths,' but he accuses such a person of coldness, unfriendliness, and crass utilitarianism. 'He is an isolated island. No outpouring of love links him with the mainland of humanity.' A third way between a 'tough mind and a tender heart' in the quest for freedom is that combination of the two that King finds in the very nature of the Christian deity:

> The greatness of our God lies in the fact that he is both toughminded and tenderhearted. He had qualities both of austerity and of gentleness. The Bible ... expresses his toughmindedness in his justice and wrath and his tenderheartedness in his love and grace. God has two outstretched arms. One is strong enough to surround us with justice, and one is gentle enough to embrace us with grace.[22]

It was inevitable that King would become a source of irritation and challenge of Joseph H. Jackson, the powerful president of the National Baptist Convention, Inc., who was not unseated from that position until 1982. Jackson represented the old-style, Bookerite leadership, essentially survivalist in character but certainly not against racial progress. This element of black Baptist leadership was rather commited to a nonconfrontational, conservative amelioration of the racial status quo. Such an orientation could only be threatened by the young Ph.D. from Crozer Theological Seminary and Boston University. Jackson took serious exception to King's strategy.

But it is also true, and points to the extraordinary character of King's pivotal leadership, that the more liberation-oriented clergy of the North: Adam C. Powell, Jr., of Harlem, Nathan Wright of the Episcopal Diocese of Newark, New Jersey, Bishop John D. Bright of the AME Church in Philadelphia, and others had their own serious questions about whether King's Southern Baptist piety was tough and worldly enough to deal with the depths of white racism in America. They supported his non-violent strategy, but were prepared to justify self-defence in an ultimate confrontation with violent white power. In that sense they expressed, in a way that King made possible but never appreciated, the subtle interpretation of the survival and liberation perspectives among certain mainline clergy in the Northern ghettos. They opened the way to the connection between the secular black power movement and black theology.

We will need a definite study of how black power and the contemporary expression of black theology closely related to it, attempted to draw out the dialectical character of black religion implied and illuminated by King's leadership. He was never prepared to acknowledge those implications, or admit that he had made a contribution to the radical rethinking of black Christianity. The new black theology, however, is grounded in the liberation tradition of one important segment of the mainline black church to which he belonged. It seeks to learn from and assimilate the values of the black consciousness form of the survival tradition that he enlisted by the appeal he made to the urban masses within and outside of the churches. The two streams point to the diverse perspective in the black theology movement today. If it still holds together such divergent points of view as that of Albert B. Cleage, Jr., Cornel West, J. Deotis Roberts, and James H. Cone, it is because this way of doing theology in the post-Civil Rights black community stands astride of both Martin Luther King, the tenderhearted liberationist, and Malcolm X, the toughminded survivalist.

In step with King, black theologians attempt to do Christian theology from a Christian social action and ecumenical perspective. In step with Malcom, they refuse to be domesticated or dominated by the norms of white Christianity. If black theology tends in one direction more than another, it perhaps leans today toward Malcolm rather than Martin. It desires to be Pan-African rather than Euro-American. It defines more with a Marxist social analysis and the liberation theologies of the Third World than with American liberalism and the neo-orthodox theology of Reinhold Niebuhr, which emphasized the insufficiency of human striving within history. It aspires more to be a theology of the people than an academic, professional theology. Its over-arching interest is in making contact with the masses and re-educating them for taking and wielding power. It understands one of its primary tasks to be the uncovering of a subteranean connection between black folk religion and the power of Ultimate Reality — the affinity between authentic spirituality and political salience that transcends the unspiritual, compromised Christianity of Europe and North America.

Black theologians generally believe that there is an alternative form of faith, drawing from the experience of black suffering and struggle, which can open up a new way of being both black and Christian. In this way, they seek to be in solidarity with struggling peoples, particularly in the Third World. They are convinced not only that no one is free until all are free, but also that it is only when people struggle for their survival and liberation that they begin to understand what it means to be human.

The future

We have finally come full circle in what essentially has been a summary and recapitulation in this chapter of the main themes and emphasis of an interpretation of black religious history shared by many black theologians today. We have seen that in the sense the development of black theology comes as a culmination of more than two centuries of struggle and resignation, rejection and affirmation, reflection and action on the part of black men and women about the relationship between their existence as a people and the truth of biblical faith. As a contribution to the discussion that has been going on for almost twenty years in black theological circles, I might dare at this point to be somewhat more subjective and indicate what I consider the starting point for more fruitful theological work in this area and a more effective praxis on the part of the black church on behalf of the poor and oppressed.

If we may presuppose the critical importance of Scripture and the witness of the early church (including, incidentally, the church in ancient Ethiopia and Nubia, which has been a neglected area of church history in the West), it should be stressed that the first source of the black theology is the black community itself. The seminal motifs or traditions we have discussed are still and continue to resist total institutionalization in the black community — merging with the church at times, but also maintaining a certain distance for it. Such traditions continue to be nurtured outside the church by a segment of the community that has never ceased to provide radical movements of resistance to white oppression whenever the institutionalized churches retreated behind a wall of complacency or fear, or in deference to an apolitical Christianity that belongs more to white evangelicalism than to black faith.

Black faith as a folk religion continued to be utilized as the motivating power for revolutionary and nationalist movements in the mass-based community. From the Ethiopian Manifesto of Robert A. Young in the early nineteenth century to Cleage's Black Christian Nationalists in the twentieth, a tenuous but persistent connection has been maintained to some of the most important elements of African and Afro-Caribbean culture. The connection, whether or not it was recognized as such by the masses, was particularly evident in nationalist cults and movements during the 1970s.[23] But it is also reflected today in more mainline developments such as the National Black Evangelical Association, the National Office of Black Catholics, the National Conference of Black Churchmen, Partners in Ecumenism, the Society for the Study of Black Religion and the Black Theology Project of Theology in the Americans.[24]

To the extent that these groups and others continue to draw their main strength from the masses, they will foster the rationalization of certain elements of Black religion toward the pursuit of freedom and social justice. Their ideological roots, however, must go down into the soil of the folk community if they are to maintain their credibility. This is why the lower-class black community must be considered one of the primary sources for the development of a black Christian theology.

Black theologians must learn to appreciate and understand these roots before turning to white scholars for the substance of their reflection on the meaning of God, human existence, and freedom. Folk religion is a constituent factor in every significant crisis in the black community. We ignore it only at the risk of being cut off from the real springs of action. When the black community is relatively integrated with white society, the folk religious elements recede from black institutions to form a hard core of unassimilable nationalism in the interstices of the social system — biding its time. When the black community is hardpressed by poverty and oppression, when hopes are crushed under the heels of resurgent racism, the essential folk elements exhibit themselves and begin once again to infiltrate the power centers that ignored or neglected them. This is the significance of the development of the 1960s that Vincent Harding called 'the religion of Black Power.' It is what lies behind the effort of many of us to create a radical theology among the grassroots clergy and laity of the contemporary black church.

A second source of black theology may be found in the writings, sermons, and addresses of the black preachers and public men and women of the past. Just as white theology has its Augustine, Calvin, Luther, and Wesley, so black theology has its David Walker, Nathaniel Paul, Richard Allen, Sojourner Truth, and W.E.B. Du Bois. We have not made as much use of the contribution of these heroes and heroines of the past as we should. Several of those names remind us that not all black thinkers for whom religion was a critical resource were members of the clergy. Nevertheless, almost all were conditioned by religious sentiments in the black community and they reflected the distinctive spirituality that is of the black religion and philosophy.[25] One cannot understand the genius of charismatic non-clerics such as Martin Delany, Marcus Garvey, Malcolm X, or James Forman without understanding how their interpretations of the black experiences were influenced by great men and women of the past who laid the foundation for Afro-American life and culture upon the bedrock of black faith.

In an important but neglected article written in 1964, Carleton Lee indicated the significance of prophecy in the black community as spiritual vision, a way of 'forth-telling' the transcedent meaning of history revealed to the inspired imagination.[26] To the extent that secular prophets draw upon the story of suffering and struggle in the community and point to the fulfilment of the faith and hope of the people, they deal with insights, motifs and traditions of the black religious consciousness. They interpret reality in ways that are either religious or can be incorporated into a basically religious view of life.

Writings of nineteenth century black philosophers and preachers disclose some of the seminal ideas of twentieth century black theology: survival, self-help, elevation, chosenness, emigration, unity, reparations, liberation. There are the religiously-charged themes with which Payne, Crummell, Henry M. Turner, and Garvey were concerned. The broad vistas of black reality that these ideas encompass need to be excavated for the richness of theological insight they contain for all people.

In 1970 James H. Cone made a beginning of this excavation by publishing a systematic theology based upon the black experience.[27] J. Deotis Roberts made a similar attempt in 1974.[28] For most part, both of these writers retained traditional categories in their early work and, therefore, found it necessary to validate their positions with arguments from white theology that would have difficulty making connection with the black experience. The use of white theological categories in black theology is certainly not to be prohibited. For there is nothing necessarily incompatible between black faith and the gospel and tradition of the early church that white theologians profess to intepret. But neither is it the only option available to us whose ancestors neither produced nor expressed an interest in the theology that came out of Rome, Wittenberg, or Geneva.[29]

Black theologians' interests should lie in another direction. What is needed to think theologically about the corpus of black philosophy — both written and oral — is a new consciousness of peoplehood and a new way of perceiving and ordering religious, cultural, and political data from the black community around the basic traditions of survival and liberation. This will, of course, require a new set of interpretive tools, a new hermeneutic. Henry H. Mitchell recognized the need of us to break with the intepretive conventions of white theology when he observed as early as 1970:

> Just as the new hermeneutic of Ebeling and others has sought to recapture the vital message of Luther and the

Reformation Fathers for the benefit of their sons, so must the Black hermeneutic seek to look into the message of the Black past and see what the Black Fathers could be saying to Black people today.[30]

Today, of course, he would add 'black mothers'. In any case, Mitchell did not develop such a hermeneutic in his twin proposals that we learn how to communicate in the folk idiom of the uneducated black Baptist preacher, and that we determine to put the gospel on a 'tell-it-like-it-is, nitty-gritty basis.'[31] The problem of creating a black hermeneutic is infinitely more difficult than that, as he subsequently acknowledged. It has to do with the intricate work of unpacking the mythology, folklore, and ethical norms of the black community as reflected in its oral tradition and literature, in order to uncover the ways in which blacks have linguistically and otherwise communicated their provisional and ultimate concerns and solutions in an exploitative and racist society. Something like what Frantz Fanon did for the people of Algeria and the French-speaking Caribbean needs to be done for oppressed blacks in the United States.[32]

Such a black hermeneutic would deal with the morphology of black English, the meaning of black music, poetry, the novel, the dance and, as Mitchell suggested, not only with the content, but the accent and cadence of black preaching. In other words, if the God of survival and liberation has identified with the struggle of black humanity and is manifest through the Afro-American experience in special ways, then we need to know more about the lifestyles and thought patterns of the community. We need to examine them through the eyes of formal and informal community leaders of the past and present. Only so shall we be able to unlock the secrets of the people's experience and develop a theology of humanization and liberation that will make contact with and be validated by that experience.

Du Bois continually reminded us that Afro-Americans have been uniquely gifted as 'a spiritual people.' There would probably be more disagreement about that bald statement today than when he wrote it. But Du Bois understood spirituality in a broader and deeper sense, not simply as a mood or disposition belonging solely to organized religion.[33] He also understood theology in a broader, nontechnical sense than is usually understood by that term today. In this nontechnical sense the theology of the black community is properly developed not exclusively in theological seminaries, but in the streets, in taverns and pool halls, as well as in churches.

The development of the first African Methodist congregation from a Free African Society, or the evolution of a nationalist organization promoting black pride from a gang of street urchins in Harlem, may more accurately reflect the operative, pragmatic spirituality and theology of the black urban community than would religious literature of all its neighbourhood Sunday schools put together. It is out of this kind of sensitivity to and knowledge of the variegated facets of black culture — the thoughts feelings, moods, and behaviour of the people of the past and the contemporary black community — that a hermeneutic can be constructed that will make it possible for theologians to formulate and read back to the community our own indigenous theology in a way that will both be recognizable by the people themselves and the basis of their self-criticism. Such a reflective and self-correcting intepretation of black religion and culture will discover that the most basic values of the community are clustered around a core of traditional beliefs and values that still include the powerful conviction that a righteous God continues to ensure human survival and justice in an inhuman and unjust world, and that this God of wrath and grace still calls the oppressed to life and liberation.

A third source of black theology is the traditional religion of Africa — a knowledge of how some of them respond to and assimilated elements of Islam and Christianity — and the concepts by which African theologians seek to make the Christian faith contextual and effective in Africa today. This is to insist that Afro-Americans are not only a spiritual people, but also an African people. We need to know what ancient and modern Africans have to contribute to our knowledge of God and the survival and liberation of the human race.

There will be differences of opinion among contemporary black intellectuals and theologians about the relevance of Africa. The academic dispute about African survivals in New World religions and cultures will persist, and many ordinary black Americans will continue to wonder what modern Africa can possibly mean to them. But it should be clear by now that blacks in the United States did not originate *ex nihilo* on the auction blocks of Charleston and New Orleans, nor should it be impossible today to help the common folk of both continents see that their experiences of capitalist exploitation and racism are too similar to be purely accidental.

The question of an American religious connection — where to renew it within the structures of the black church and how to justify it — may be more difficult. But it is possible and desirable to try to cover some of the great and enduring values of the traditional religions of Africa for the revitalization of Afro-American religion in the United States. American Christianity as a whole may be expected to share the benefits of such an exploration of African religions and philosophy, but only the theologians of the black churches may reasonably be expected to take such an initiative seriously and do something with it.

The continued development and modification of African religious beliefs and practices certainly can be traced to the islands of the Carribean and the mainland of North America. Although it is true that their contributions to our understanding of spiritual reality have all but evaporated from the patina of Afro-America Christianity, the fact remains that we do not have a sufficient understanding of contemporary black faith or the black psyche that which Jungians would call the collective unconscious of the Afro-American ethnic group — to be absolutely certain that nothing can be salvaged that could reinforce and be reinforced by the belief structures and worship practices adhered to today in Accra, Lagos, or Soweto. It would appear, even from casual observation, that some significant connections can be made, and black anthropologists and sociologists need to work with theologians to help us understand what is going on and how resources of the ancestral religions can be used to enhance the solidarity and collaboration of African and Afro-American peoples. Inasmuch as both people fought for their humanity against the military and economic power of imperialist and racist white societies, we need to share jointly in any examination of the meaning of religion and its contributions to the struggle for freedom — contributions arising out of different cultural milliex, but nevertheless containing many similar purposes and functions. The value of such collaboration among black intellectuals in the United States and between them and colleagues in Africa and the Carribean would be incalculable.

Charles Long, making a similar point, has helpfully observed:
> Our colleague Mircea Eliade said long ago that the West was in danger of provincialism through a lack of attention to the orientations and solutions of non-Western man. It would be difficult, if not impossible, to make the case for the non-Western identity of the black community in America, though several make this claim. The element of truth in this claim is that though we are Westerners, we are not Western in the same way as our compatriots, and thus we afford within American an entree to the *otherness* of America and the otherness of mankind.[34]

To what do we refer when we speak of the valuable contributions of African religion? Among other emphases, a profound sense of the pervasive reality of the spirit world above and beneath the artifactual world; the blotting out of line between the sacred and profane; the practical use of religion in all of life; the surrender of excessive individualism for solidarity with the community and with nature; reverence for the ancestors and their real and symbolic presence with the living to guide and inspire; the source of evil in the consequence of an act rather than in the act itself; the corporateness of society and all life; the creative employment of rhythm, singing, and dancing in the celebration of life and the worship of the Creator.

All these elements of African traditional religions were found in some form, however attenuated, in the slave community of the eighteenth and nineteenth centuries and were absorbed to some degree into Christianity in the Carribean and North America. It should be noted that many of them are also found in Amerindian religions and some attempt is being made to recover them from that source. But it was mainly in the development of the religion of the African slaves in the United States that a major effort was made by whites to nullify all African influences and substitute Euro-American religious norms and conventions. Black Americans, nevertheless, persisted in religious beliefs and practices that defied total assimilation.

The emotionality, spontaneity, and freedom of black faith has much to do with the instinctive resistance of Afro-Americans to absolute whitenization, but that resistance is also related to the intrinsic discontinuity between African and European spirituality, not altogether resolved by evangelization. Black theologians cannot continue to ignore these points of discontinuity if they want to make a distinctive contribution to the black church and to American religion in general. We have a great deal more work to do on both sides of the Atlantic if we are genuinely interested in the recovery and enhancement of values, particularly those that reflect the affirmation of life — at a time when whites seem bent upon their own destruction, and with them everyone else in the world — the unity of all life in the unquenchable desire for liberation, the freedom to be *Muntu,* man and woman, in the most penetrating sense of that profound Bantu word.

The theological program of African scholars, for example in the All Africa Conference of Churches, to Africanize Christianity has much to say to black theologians' attempts to indigenize the Christian faith in the culture of black America. In both instances the purpose should not be handed for the imposition of white Christianity in black vesture upon the unsuspecting masses in Africa and America. On the contrary, it should be a sincere effort to grasp a new revelation of old truths, to unveil the reality of Jesus Christ the Liberator in the life and destiny of the black world.

Related to such an effort are the urgent political issues of liberation in Southern Africa and in the United States, social justice for the masses, true development in independent Africa, the relationship of black Christianity to the separatist or independent, prophet-led churches on both sides of the Atlantic, and the contribution of the churches of Africa and black America to the ongoing revolutions of the Third World. Only sympathetic and intensive dialogue among theologians in Africa, the Carribeans, and North America will be able to expose the harmonies and disharmonies in black religious development on an intercontinental basis and forge theological and ideological linkages that can bind modern Africa and black America together for the enormous possibilies of the future.

We can only hope that the black world, once it has gained its long denied power, will not repeat the errors of the white world. It is not altogether self-evident from this study that we blacks will escape that fate, but it is, as Du Bois wrote, 'a thing of questing for eternal youth, of fruitful labor, of joy and music, of the free spirit and of the ministering hand.' If we are vindicated in this hope, reconcilliation between old enemies and estranged peoples will be the eschatological event that all of us await with eager longing.

The gift of faith was wrought out of the distinctive way God was revealed to pre-colonial Africa and it was shaped, for five hundred years, by the experience of suffering and struggle related to oppression. Its lasting contribution will be its demonstration of what it takes for a people to survive and achieve inner and external liberation under the strange circumstances of being downtrodden under the heel of Christian racists. Perhaps for that very reason the future of Christianity in Africa and in the diasporic communities of people of African descent may be to provide a bridge for First world Christians and non-Christians in the rest of the world to come together around the universal yearning for *shalom* — the justice, wholeness, peace, and healing that transcends any one religious vision and belongs to the whole human family.

The joyous testimony of the men and women whose tortured footsteps we have followed through the history of America has been to 'keep on keeping on,' as Fannie Lou Hamer used to say, 'down the freedom road' — to continue, in other words, the struggle which refuses to settle for anything less than total liberation for the total creation. That has been black folks' answer to that mysterious question of Jesus in Luke 18:8 — 'Nevertheless, when the Son of man comes, will he find faith on the earth?'

FOOTNOTES

1. Eugene D Genovese, *Roll Jordan, Roll: The World the Slaves Made* (New York: Pantheon, 1974, p.91)
2. In addition to Genovese (note 1, above), see John W. Blassingame, *The Slave Community: Plantation Life in the Antebellum South* (New York: Oxford University Press, 1972); Henry H Mitchell, *Black Belief: Folk Belies of Blacks in America and West Africa* (New York: Harper & Row, 1975); Lawrence W Levine, *Black Culture and Black Consciousness: Afro-American Folk Thought from Slavery to Freedom* (New York: Oxford University Press, 1978); Albert J Raboteau, Slave Religion: *The 'Invisible Institution' in the Antebellum South* (New York: Oxford University Press); and George E Simpson, *Black Religions in the New World* (Columbia University Press, 1978).
3. See Mechal Sobel, Travellin' On: *The Slave Journey to an Afro-Baptist Faith* (Westtport, Conn.: Greenwood, 1979), pp,99-135.
4. See, e.g., Willis D Wetherford, *American Churches and the Negro* (Boston: Christopher Publ. House, 1957), and Carter G Woodson, *The History of the Negro Church* (Washington, D C: Associated Publishers, 1972).
5. John Lovell, Jr., Black Song: *The Forge and the Flame* (New York: Macmillan, 1972), p.229.
6. St Clair Drake and Horace R Cayton, Black Metropolis: *A Study of Negro Life in a Northern City* (New York: Harcourt, Brace, 1945), pp.650-57.
7. C Eric Lincoln, *The Black Muslims in America* (Boston: Beacon, 1961), pp.217-20.
8. Sterling Brown, Arthur P Davis, and Ulysses Lee, *The Negro Caravan* (New York: Arno Press and the New York Times, 1941), p.422.
9. W E B Du Bois, *The Souls of Black Folk* (Greenwich, Conn.: Fawett, 1961), p.149.
10. Ibid.

11. Lawrence W Levine, *Black Culture and Black Consciousness* (New York: Oxford University Press, 1977), p.80.
12. Du Bois, *Souls*, p.151.
13. See Leonard E Barrett, *Soul-Force: African Heritage in Afro-American Religion* (Garden City, NY: Doubleday, 1974), p.115.
14. Langstone Hughes, in Francis Broderick et.al., *Black Protest Thought in the Twentieth Century* (New York: Bobbs Merrill, 1970), p.92.
15. Derek Walcott, in Orde Coombs, *Is Massa Day Dead? Black Moods in the Carribean* (Garden City, N Y: Doubleday, 1974), p.7.
16. Blassingame, *The Slave Community*, pp.205-6.
17. William Hammilton, 'An Address to the New York African Society for Mutual Relief,' in Dorothy Porter, ed., *Early Negro Writing, 1760-1837* (Boston: Beacon, 1971), p.37.
18. Ibid., 'Minutes and Proceedings of the First Annual Meeting of the American Moral Reform Society,' p207.
19. E.Franklin Frazier, *The Negro Church in America* (New York: Schocken, 1964), p.86.
20. I refer to the Colored Primitive Baptist (1865), the reunited African Methodists (1866), the Second Cumberland Presbyterians (1869), and the Colored Methodist Episcopal Church, of which considerably more is known, founded in 1870. Among the Holiness and Pentecostal churches of the period were William Christian's Church of the living God (1889), C H Mason's Church of God in Christ (1895), and William Crowdy's Church of God and Saints of Christ, founded in 1896.
21. Black consciousness, if not political militancy, appeared at various times in the Church of God and Saints of Christ, the Church of the Living God, the early Garveyite African Orthodox Church, and in the Black Muslim movement.
22. Martin Luther King, Jr, *Strength to Love* (Cleveland: Collins World, 1953), p.15

23. Some of the publicized examples were movements led by Armiri Baraka, Ron Karenga, Milton Henry, Brother Imari of the Republic of New Africa, and Albert B. Cleage of the Shrine of the Black Madonna.
24. See representative statements in Gayraud S Wilmore and James H. Cone, *Black Theology: A Documentary History* (Maryknoll, N Y, Orbis 1979).
25. For a study of philosophy in the black community and its relationship to folk religious beliefs, see Denis Hickey, *Contemporary Black Philosophy* (Pasadena: Williams and Williams, 1791). An important new work linking Marxist philosophy and black theology is Cornel West, *Prophesy and Deliverance!* An Afro-American Revolutionary Christianity (Phila.: Westminister Press, 1982).
26. Carleton L Lee, 'Religious Roots of the Negro Protest,' in Arnold Rose, ed., *Assuring Freedom to the Free* (Detroit: Wayne State University Press, 1964).
27. James H Cone, *A Black Theology of Liberation* (Philadelphia: Lippincott, 1970).
28. J Deotis Roberts, *A Black Political Theology* (Philadelphia: Westminister, 1974).
29. See Cecil W. Cone, *The Identity Crisis in Black Theology* (Nashville: A M E C Press, 1975), pp.138-44.
30. Henry H Mitchell, *Black Preaching* (Philadelphia: Lippincott, 1970), p.27.
31. ibid., pp.29-31.
32. See, e.g., Frantz Fanon, *Black Skin, White Masks* (New York: Grove, 1967).
33. See Herbert Aptheker, ed., W E B Du Bois — *Prayers for Dark People* (University of Massachussets Press, 1980).
34. Charles H Long, 'The Black Reality: Toward a Theology of Freedom,' in *Criterion*, Journal of the University of Chicago Divinity School, Sept 1969

2

The Socio-Cultural Analysis of the Origins and Development of Black Theology

Cecil Mzingisi Ngcokovane

For almost two decades, Black Theology has sought definitions of itself and has not succesfully outgrown such a stage. Hence a Black Theology Conference held in Wilgespruit, South Africa, on 16-19 August 1983, felt the need and urgency to move out of such an impasse.[1] The consensus reached, which combined contemporary viewpoint, is that Black theologians should now address themselves, *inter alia*, to the content of Black Theology and its methodology.[2]

There are of course some South African Black theologians, who might argue that such a notion is historically incorrect, in that there is already published material which has been trying to deal with the subject matter of Black Theology. They will point out, for example that there are articles which have been published on Christology, on the whole question of the theology of labour, of anthropology and so on. I agree that, to a certain extent, there are a few scholars such as Maimela and Mofokeng who have not approached their work from a definitional standpoint.

But my contention is that, besides such isolated cases here and there, Black South African theologians have historically been trying to justify themselves; battling to find a place for the legitimacy of Black Theology in the sphere of traditional theology. It is this kind of capacity to definition and justification that I am talking about. This captivity is also true (to a certain extent) of some black theologians in North America.

For me, the crucial question is, why should we keep on justifying ourselves instead of looking at the problem from our own perspective - a perspective which is informed by our faith and our black experience. My faith, for example, is not informed by the 'visible church' which, in all it does and says, is informed by beliefs/ideas which are rooted in the Western cultural ideology. Rather, my faith is informed by what could be called the 'invisible church' or the 'understructure church', that is to say, a certain type of church within the institutional church. This is the kind of church where my ancestors and my parents have found themselves.

Beyond, if not within, the definitional stance of Black theologians, there is a problem with regard to conceptual tools of analysis. Black theologians have, hitherto, employed race analysis in their theological reflection. But the crucial question to be raised is:

To what extent is the racialistic conceptual analysis adequate for the understanding of problems of Blacks in South Africa, North America, the African continent and the rest of the world? I will focus this question on South Africa in order to be contextual in my approach to the topic under consideration.

I would like to argue that any socio-cultural analysis of the origins and development of Black Theology in the world, especially in South Africa, must of necessity seriously take into account the historical, materialist background. Therefore, the purpose of this paper is not to dismiss the tools which have been used for a discourse on Black theology so far. Rather, it is to find out whether such tools of analysis cannot be extended to deal with the reality of political economy of race and class in God's world. Thus an adequate socio-cultural analysis of the origins and development of Black theology needs to take such an approach as one of the starting points.

Both the content and methodology of Black Theology in South Africa has not seriously taken into account the exploitation of African labour. The object of this paper is to show why and how this labour was and continues to be exploited. Thus I am more interested in the relations between the socio-cultural facts of exploitation of blacks as members of the working class and as peasants. I would also like to show how such facts influence the development of racism in our land.

I regard the identification of casual relations as a key to an adequate explanation of how racism developed to become what it is in South Africa today and how such a development has, in turn, given rise to Black Theology. Moreover, I would like to probe into the reasons why the origins and development of Black Theology have not dealt with question of black labour exploitation.

The Problem and its Matrix: Towards a Theoretical Framework

According to R Turner, most people make choices within a very narrow context, defined by a set of implicit socio-cultural, religious and economic values which they do not realise can themselves be chosen or rejected. Black Christians and their theologians have been victims of such blind choices.[3] They have been victimised by a religion (Christianity) with Western theological pressupositions that are rooted in the Euro-American cultural ideology. At the bottom of such a cultural ideology are the Western capitalist and imperialist interests. How is it that Black Theology has not been able to unmask such latent presuppositions? I will come back to this question later.

A close look at the socialisation process will help us understand the problem faced by Black theologians today. I agree with Turner that socialisation prepares people not just for social living, but for living out specific roles in specific social structures. Hence Turner contends that:

> The social structure may be one of gross inequality, but if the socialisation mechanisms are working effectively the independent kicking child can be turned into the passive, accepting adult at the bottom of the pile, who accepts he/she has been deprived of the capacity to conceive of any other way of existing. That is, the effect of the process of socialisation is to make a particular social structure and a particular human model seem to be natural, and to hide the fact that it is not natural, and could be changed.[4]

Indeed, Turner is correct when he contends that the process of socialisation can thus narrow a person's range or perceptions and choices to a predefined social reality.[5] It is such an ideological-cultural captivity that the Church in the 'Black world' finds itself. Black Theology needs to shake loose of such captivity in its theological reflection. Black theologians ought to uncover how socialisation processes can induce acceptance of inequality by the oppressed masses in an unjust sociaty. Black theologians must unmask those latent socio-cultural and ideological forces that make the oppressed masses come to believe in their "own" inferiority and in the natural rights of their exploiters and oppressors. How such blind acceptance of inequalities works has been clearly pointed out by Turner when he says that:

> This is not something necessarily brought about by the Machiavellian cunning of the dominant group. Once a social structure is in existence, mechanisms take over which tend to keep it going. The dominant groups are also being socialised. They are socialised into dominant roles, with the concomitant belief in the naturalness of their dominance, of their superiority, whether it be race superriority in South Africa, caste superiority in classical India, or the superior virtues and intelligence of the middle classes in the 19th century Europe. The system seems to perpetuate itself ...[6]

In South Africa, a social structure such as the one mentioned in the above statement is perpetuated by capitalism. Turner correctly points out that the human model characteristic of the dominant white group in South Africa is the capitalist human model. He also contends that the value imposed by the socialisation process in capitalist societies are those that particular form of society needs in order to survive.[7] Turner identifies some essential elements of capitalist society as follows:

1. 'Some people control the means of production. The rest of the population, having no tools or land of their own, have no

option but to work for those who do own tools or the land. And the owners naturally expect to get something out of permitting them to do so. The basis upon which they are employed is that some of the products of their labour should be given to the capitalist's means of production. To put it another way, the worker receives wages that are less than the value of his/her labour. The capitalist accumulates capital by taking the surplus product, which he/she has not produced. This is exploitation ...

2. The capitalist's objective in exploiting workers is not, as might be expected, simply for their own personal good, in terms of a comfortable life and high level of consumption. If it were, they would, once they had made their first million, retire, relax and enjoy themselves. But they do not. They ruin their health competing for a level of wealth which they could not possibly consume, even if they wanted to.[8]

Capitalists continue to accumulate because for them, accumulation becomes an end in itself instead of being a means to an end. Such an activity results in the social system becoming an independent thing and people becoming subject to it.[9] This leads to Turner's third essential element of capitalist society, namely, that:

3. At an advanced level of accumulation, the need for markets as an outlet for the products of all this accumulated capital becomes important. It therefore becomes necessary to boost the consumption of that sector of the population which has surplus cash. They have to be forced to consume the product, whether they 'want' to or not ... This role played by advertising ... This forced consumption can occur among certain social groups at the same time as other groups are being forced to restrict consumption by being paid low wages so that their employers can accumulate more.[10]

If one were to use J Habermas expression of labour, one would content that labour is a fundamental category of human existence.[11] Hence Buti Tlhagale, drawing upon Gregory Baum, could say that:

> Through labour (people) transform nature. Through labour human beings build their environment, their world and in so doing they simultaneously build themselves. In a collective labour engagement, (people) build themselves together. Thus (people) in their collective labouring efforts become co-creators. They are the effective subjects of what they create.[12]

Such a conception of labour is ideally sound, but the capitalist system upset the whole scheme of co-creation. How such a process takes place, has been well articulated by Turner when he says that:

> In (a capitalist) society, acquisition, ownership and consumption of material goods is the greatest aim of human beings. Work is only a means to this.
> It is not something an individual does because of the inherent meaningfulness of creative activity. It is an unpleasant necessity to be got over as soon as possible so that you can go home and consume.[13]

The meaning of this statement is that the worker is a means for the capitalist's end of accumulating. Hence Turner contends that work is often objective as unpleasant as it is described to be.

> The capitalist employs the worker for an objective other than the worker's own satisfaction, so the nature of the work and the work environment are designed for that other purpose. They are designed to maximise profit, not to give the worker satisfaction from a meaningful task.[14]

Blacks, both in the USA and in the 'Republic' of South Africa are victims of such an economic system. However, Black theologians are still hesitant to take a plunge and vigorously attack this issue head on. Hence the origins and development of Black Theology have been extremely lacking in this regard. I shall now look at how the capitalist system and its values have actually influenced theological reflection in capitalist societies such as the

USA, SA and Western Europe. Imbued by Western capitalist and cultural values, the carriers of Christianity have, in turn, influenced theological discourse among Black theologians.

To understand this process, we need to take a close look at cultural domination in a particular context, for example, South Africa, and also at an ethical system that places limitations on human community.

Conquest and Cultural Domination

Bernard Magubane has correctly pointed out that the supremacy of the whites, their values and civilisation, was only won when the cultural and value system of the defeated African was reduced to nothing and when the Africans themselves loudly admitted the cultural hegemony of their conquerors.[15] Such a notion became also true in the religious sphere.

Christianity carriers in it, *inter alia*, two kinds of ethical system. According to Turner, one kind accepts the predominant human model and tries to rationalise it, to smooth the edges. Turner calls such an ethical system an 'internal morality' which he articulates as follows:

> ... pay our debts, give to the poor,
> don't tell lies, don't steal (i.e. don't deprive people of property which is theirs in terms of the given legal property system in ways that the system does not permit).
> In a slave society, feed your slaves properly, don't sell their children until they are eight years old. In war, kill people with bullets, but not with poison gas.[16]

Such an ethic justifies or legitimises institutionalised violence, racism and economic exploitation. But it also does more. It creates passivity on the part of the victims of such a system and also imbues them with a sense of guilt whenever they question such unethical values. Consequently, they accept such an ethical system as a given axiom not to be challenged. Hence the exploited and the oppressed find themselves in a vicious cycle of pain. This kind of ethical system also makes life easier for people within the system who find themselves not challenging the human model implicit in the system. Black theologians are constantly haunted by this kind of ethical system.

Although Black theologians employ the second kind of ethical system, namely 'transcendent morality' in their theological reflection, they nonetheless fall short of their essential task. Transcendent morality is defined by Turner as:

> (An ethical system which) goes beyond the given and ask the fundamental question - what is human life for, what is the meaning of human life?[17]

It is an ethic which challenges the human model implicit in the system. The 'transcendent ethic' - demands that we question our taken-for-granted ways of behaving, that we continually need to question them. It is on the basis of 'transcendent ethic' that Black theologians, like other religious leaders, have continually attacked both old religious forms and social forms. They have attacked religious forms which have, in fact, lost their transcendence and which have instead become merely repetitive. Black theologians have attacked social forms which have become unquestioned, mechanical, and non-human and unjust, hence dehumanising.[18] But such an attack is now new because we find it in Hebrew prophets, Jesus Christ and Muhammad. Such a view is best articulated by Turner when he contends that:

> We have seen the Hebrew prophets attacking the worship of the Golden Calf — both an idol with a ritual attached, and a way of life in which personal material satisfaction turns one away from one's neighbour. We have seen Christ breaking the Sabbath to cure the sick - so showing that the material ritual of Sabbath observance must give way to an intelligent understanding of the transcendent significance of the Sabbath as a day in which I cease from my own selfish pursuits and consider the needs of the whole, and hence of other men and women. We have Muhammad challenging the way of the wealthy merchants

of Mecca, who believed that their wealth gave them power over both people and gods, by asserting the universality of the one God, who cannot be bought, and by asserting that wealth must be used for social purposes, not for individual purposes.[19]

However, the history of religion shows us that it is one of gradual decline of such transcendent beliefs and practices into the given, 'a decline whereby they become nothing more than a traditional way of life' in which religious observance is mere ritual and in which the transcendent ethic gets moulded into the very untrascendental social structure, and becomes an 'opium of the people'; until a new reformer shatters the structure, either by creating a new religion (Muhammad), or by appealing to the pristine transcendence of an earlier religious genius (Calvin).[20]

Nevertheless, the social relevance of religion does not only lie in the fact that it commands us to question accepted human models and the accepted social structure in which they are embodied, but also lies in the clinical examination of such accepted human models and social structures.

Thus I J Mosala has criticised Black theologians of being blind to the fact that in their attack/criticism of 'White Theology', they are actually using the same tools of analysis that whites have traditionally used to justify their case. According to Mosala, while Black Theology has advocated black liberation and the black experience as a focus in its analysis it has continued to draw its biblical hermeneutical assumptions from White Theology. Mosala's strongest point is that Black Theology does this irrespective of the class character of the Bible. In doing this, Mosala slashes J Cone, C West, A Boesak, S Gqubule, E Mgojo, S Dwane, and M Buthelezi.[21]

C West, for example has long claimed that Black Theology and Marxist thought share three characteristics as follows:

1. Both adhere to similar methodology, the same way of approaching their respective subject matter and arriving at conclusions.

2. Both link some notion of liberation to some future socio-economic condition of the down-trodden.
3. And this is most important, both attempt to put forward trenchant critiques of liberal capitalist America.[22]

For C West, Black theologians and Marxist thinkers need to preserve their own existential and intellectual integrity and explore the possibility of promoting fundamental social amelioration together.[23] While Mosala has raised a thought-provoking criticism, one begins to realise the need to ask him the question: What tools of analysis is he using? Who has given him and other Black theologians (including myself) the right to theologise about the black working class and black peasants if we are not part of their struggle? Have the poor, the oppressed and black working class given us the mandate to do theology about them? What does the record show in terms of our daily participation in the struggle of black people?

When I question Mosala about the tools of analysis that he is using, I am conscious of the fact that in this paper I am using the same tools (materialist/marxist). I have no more problem with his tools than I have a problem with his indictment of Black theologians. He contends that Black theologians in South Africa and in the United States suffer from uncritical use of Western paradigms and yet he focuses (as is the case with my paper) on marxist paradigms which are also Western without being critical of them too. I think that the problem at stake here is that of Black theological bankrupcy.

It is because of black intellectual bankruptcy that one finds oneself caught up in the middle, especially when one is dealing with material questions. There have been those grand schemes (i.e. capitalism and socialism) that have for so long affected the world. And one has to come to grips with that reality and make a choice. In fact, I find something very African in the marxist paradigm which I do not find in the categories of capitalism.

What I find in the marxist notion of historical dialectical materialism is a concern about class. If you look at African communalism, although you will find classes, there was a sense by which you could talk of a classless society, for example, what is idiomatically called *'Inkomo ye Nqoma yi Ntswengw'e Bheka'* has inherent in it a sense of socialism where some people cannot afford to enjoy luxuries when others lack necessities. Here I am not saying communalism is marxism but that I can identify with some aspects of the latter which are actually part and parcel of my own heritage and experience. In African communalism, there will be no person in the community who will stay without a piece of land to till, even if that person does not 'own' a piece of land. This is Africa before colonialism and her conquest by the West.

In pre-colonial Africa there were elements, that I identify, which took seriously the question of disparity between the haves and the have-nots. You would get a cow, for example, which I have called *'Inkomo ye Nqoma'* (i.e. borrowed cow). A person did not need to borrow it but someone would give the cow to you on a loan basis which does not mean that if the cow dies you should pay the 'owner'. But if it continues to live and bear calves, you keep it as long as the owner has not come for it. But you always know, that it's not yours. When the owner comes for it, you keep the offspring. Thus you end up with cattle which you would not have otherwise. Thus in African communalism, one could not stay hungry when others have plenty.

B Tlhagale contends that:

> If Black theology is to talk meaningfully about Christian symbols and how they affect the socio-economic conditions of the Black people, it will have to grapple with the fundamental contradictions that explain the nature of the present society.[24]

If the historical materialistic background is not seriously taken into account by Black theologians, Black theology, as in the past, would be done in a vacuum. Hence the need for Black theologians to boldly unmask the falsehood of White Theology with its cultural ideology in a manner that will clinically deal with the question of the political economy of race and class, not only in South Africa, but throughout the world. Thus, Black theology in its development, needs to outgrow the two kinds of ethical system which I mentioned earlier on (i.e 'internal morality' and 'transcendent ethic').

Conclusion

Black theology both in its origins and development has been held in capacity by a theology which is grounded in Euro-American capitalist interest and cultural values - theology that has never given room to the democratilisation of the Church structure (as an institution) and theological enterprise. Thus democratisation can only be done by and/or with the masses themselves. Here I am talking about 'people's theology' and /or 'ministry by the people'. The starting point for such a ministry or theology is a sober look, and clinical criticism of the present theological captivity in which Black theologians find themselves.

Indeed, such a starting point will constitute a realistic vision for the future of Black theology. Since theology is done within the confines of a Euro-American cultural ideology and capitalist interests, Black theology must now begin to consider the notion of democratisation seriously. This will be a new stage - a stage when the masses assume full control of their lives in all spheres of life, especially the religious life.

One of the problems of capitalist societies and their Churches, is that they allow democratisation only in the sphere of politics or the state and deny the masses of society democratic participation in the economic sphere. This is due to the notion of the maintenance of the sanctity of private property in the means of production. Thus there is democracy in the political sphere and lack of democracy in the economic sphere. Consequently, the dominant theologies of the Euro-American traditions are bound up in such a captivity and, in turn, such a captivity has affected Black theology.

The lack of democracy in the economic sphere, that is to say, the black working masses not having their own representatives, and participation in the decision-making corporate bodies, and the lack of democracy in the political sphere, consequently create the pattern for the lack of democracy for the black working masses in all other institutions of society, including the Church and its seminaries.

The biggest problem Black Christians face in an undemocratic, bureaucratic society, such as South Africa, is that theology is designed and controlled by a white group ruling over blacks. Since South African society is one that is characterised by racial and class oppressions, all theology for the oppressed group of lower classes is irrelevant because it is designed and controlled by a group other than the oppressed themselves. Hence theology in a situation of class and racial oppression tends to justify the existing socio-cultural, political and economic inequalities. Theology, therefore, has perpetuated ignorance and acceptance of the system on the part of blacks in the world. It is precisely at this point that a black theologian has need of a stern theological education from the people below. This is the basis of the demand for 'people's theology' or 'ministry by the people'.

I know that some folks argue that to speak of 'people's theology' is idealistic. Such people tend to raise the following question: Why should the so-called people be canonised to be the only legitimate voice to be listened to? Are we calling for some type of dialogue between the intellectuals and the people - the oppressed, or are we saying that intellectuals must shut up because they have been talking too much? But it must be understood that I am not suggesting there should be no guiding principles from intellectuals in the people's struggle. What I am saying is that intellectuals cannot do theology without becoming concretely involved in the struggle for freedom and justice.

I contend that we need to close the gap between where people/the masses are, and where theologians tend to do their theological imaginings. I agree with the position of the Institute for Contextual Theology that there are times when we need to go out of our studies into places where there is development; where there is experience; and where people have got their own stories to tell. It is an opportunity that intellectuals will find too costly if they let it pass them by. When theologians/intellectuals come down from 'ivory towers' to where people are, they find themselves being part of the masses, and part of the masses experience stories. Such experiences and stories will form the basis upon which the intellectuals begin formulating the guiding principles for the people's struggle.

Black Theology to be worth its name must of necessity be informed, *inter alia*, by the black people's experiences (materially and ideologically). This is the point that I am trying to make here. But at the same time, I am saying that there should be no intellectuals to do theological reflection. Nonetheless there should be some type of concrete dialogue and interaction between the intellectuals and the people - the oppressed. Failure to do so will be counterproductive in the struggle for freedom. Historically, there is ample evidence for such a thesis. Let us use the French Revolution and the Peasant Revolt as some of the examples in history.

During the French Revolution, for example, the intellectuals formulated grand ideas, schemes and slogans that sounded so good and meaningful to the people - the masses in the struggle for democratic values of freedom, justice and equality. But such formulations were done in 'ivory towers' and not within the context of the suffering masses. The suffering masses took them at face value and were inspired by such ideas. They immediately got themselves engaged in a revolution without using such ideas as guiding principles due to lack of understanding of what they really meant. Thus intellectuals failed to interact with the masses at the level of meaning of such ideas on the one hand, and the masses failed to properly understand the meaning behind such grand ideas on the other. The latter became inspired without proper understanding and simply acted. All that, among other things, contributed to the failure of the French Revolution.

We can also look at the peasants' revolt in Germany and find parallels there. M. Luther's ideas inspired the peasants. But the peasants did not understand his tools of analysis. They did not understand, for example, the tension that is inherent in Luther's theological reflection, that is to say, the notion of the 'heavenly kingdom' and the 'earthly kingdom'; the 'spiritual law' and the 'human law' and so on, which, according to Luther, should not be confused. The peasants used Luther's notion of 'spiritual law' to fight against 'human law'. Luther turned against them for using the 'spiritual law' in challenging 'human law' in a head on collision. Hence their struggle failed. History will repeat itself if black intellectuals do not concretely interact with black masses in a meaningful way. I contend that the Black theological liberation project both in South Africa and in the USA must not be alienated from its matrix or from its base. How do black theologians, for example, view the sacrificial dimension of the unarticulated prophetic message of the black American ghetto youth who are willing to stand by their dead colleagues even to a point of demanding that they be killed too? Hence there is need for 'people's theology'.

In South Africa, for example, 'people's theology' must include the following elements: A clinical examination and critique of traditional Western theology in the light of the issues addressed by the KAIROS document and contextual theologies that have emerged; a reflection on the South African political, economic and educational situation and its international dimensions; and a reflection on one's perception of one's faith and experiences inside and outside the Church. There must be a thorough democratisation of the theological system with the Church providing funds and equipment as well as minimum control over theological education.

The church can also provide general guidelines which will, of course, be formulated by people themselves based on their own daily experiences and faith. Such an approach to theology, will enable Black theologians to realise that beyond racism lies the economic question. The dynamic forces which are operative in the capitalist economic system can be best understood only when Black theologians interact and listen to the Black labour force. Only when oppressed black masses control and design their theological education and seminaries, can we even begin to talk about a curriculum and philosophy of theological education. But at the heart of all this, is the economic question, without which our theology is bound to be wide off the mark. Thus our theological reflection will fizzle out and die before we start.

FOOTNOTES

1. See Conference Report entitled: *'Black Theology revisited,'* sponsored jointly by The Institute for Contextual Theology and New Horizon Project, Wilgespruit, 16 - 19 August 1983, p1.
2. Ibid
3. R Turner, 1972 *The Eye of a Needle,* p10 Braamfontein Christian Institute.
4. Ibid, p11
5. Ibid
6. Ibid
7. Ibid, p12
8. Ibid, pp13 -14
9. Ibid, p14
10. Ibid, pp14 - 15
11. J J Habermas, 1972 *Knowledge and Human Interests,* p25 London: Heinemann.
12. Conference Report on Black Theology, op.cit, p25.
13. Turner, R op cit. 15
14. B M Magubane, 1979 *The Political Economy of race and Class in South Africa*, New York; Monthly review Press.
15. Turner, op cit, p17
16. Ibid, p18
17. Ibid
18. Ibid
19. Ibid, pp 18 - 19
20. c.f. I J Mosala, 'The use of the Bible in Black Theology' I J Mosala, and B Tlhagale, (eds) *Unquestionable Right to be Free,* Skotaville Publishers, pp175 -196.
21. C West, 1979 'Black Theology and Marxist Thought' in Black Theology: *A Documentary History*, 1966 - 1979, by G Wilmore & Cone (eds), Maryknoll; Orbis books, p553.
22. Ibid
23. B Tlhagale, *'Towards a Black Theology of labour'* in Conference Report on Black Theology, op cit, p25.

3

Black Feminist Theology in South Africa

Rev. Roxanne Jordan

Creation and Black Experience

When God created the earth, the human being — both male and female — was created in God's image. God then gave both of them dominion over all the earth. This very, very fundamental biblical account of the story of creation gives the human being a tremendous sense of power and responsibility. This power to rule over all the earth has imbedded in its very essence the nature of responsible people. Surely God could not offer the earth with all its beauty and splendor without realizing that, in order to maintain the grandeur of creation without becoming self-centered, selfish, oppressive and exploitative, it would take responsible people to exercise authority. At the moment of creation, we are supposed to be crowned with this responsible oversight.

However, because of what I believe to be some irresponsible act in the Garden of Eden, authority has been usurped. And for greed and disobedience, the human race has a history of wars, all clamouring for power one over and against the other. People take captives, reduce them to slaves and servants, and dump them in prison cells, left to be forgotten. People take the captives' land and force them to work as laborers on their own (i.e., the captives') land. More often than not, the slaves and the captives, who are also commissioned by God to have dominion over all the earth, do not have enough strength to wipe from their parched lips a dirty fly. God then appeared in human flesh to restore to the oppressed people a hope for liberation in the form of Jesus Christ to set all of us, both men and women, free. God made us to be human beings. And he made us to love accordingly and to have life abundantly.

Being black, this whole ordination of human beings in creation does not seem to be intended for black South Africa. For more than three hundred years now, black people in South Africa have been brutally forced to live as aliens in their own land. The land was stolen from them. Consequently, they were subjugated to become slaves under a master on their own land. This master class of whites also brought along with them a religion *named* Christianity. However, what they taught and lived was not the Christianity of the Christ who had come to set the captives free but rather one that wanted black people to be submissive to these bosses, and one that indoctrinated us to believe we were inferior beings. Thus whites tried to reduce us to nothingness. Thank God we as black people have the spirit of liberation born right within us; we shall never be reduced to nothingness. On the contrary, out of what the white masters believed would reduce us to nothingness came a theology speaking to the situation and lives of the oppressed and exploited, giving real and concrete hope to us: black theology came forth.

Being black is synonymous with being oppressed and being exploited. In South Africa, and in all other places in the world, it means to earn less than what is humanly sufficient to eat, to be housed, and to be schooled properly. It is to see the desolation and hopelessness all around you but never to give up hope. To be black is to experience total disbelief in the face of army rifles and the military, but not to be silenced by this fear and keep on believing. To be black in South Africa is to smell the stench of injustice from the armpits of mine workers, of domestic servants, and of factory workers. To be black is to be faced very often by a board stating 'whites only' to a very beautiful park, and not to feel your humanness diminished. It is to be thrown into prison for saying that you cannot and never will stand under the authority of an unjust system; and being prepared to be imprisoned without ever standing trial.

Furthermore, it is being employed in backbreaking, low paying jobs or never to have a job, but still to have the inborn desire to want to work. In South Africa, it is to see a pregnant woman and a four-year-old child killed in cold blood by South African riot police; shots ripping through their bodies, but not giving up the fight. It is to be restricted in your movements, in your speech, in your worship, but still have the freedom to sing the Lord's song. It is to be uprooted from your dwelling place and to be placed in temporary tents, having your family wiped out in the cold face of death by the cold of the night but still have the warm will to live. It is being. It is black. It is living.

Moreover, added to this atrocious way of life is the position of the oppressed and exploited black woman in her own community. Admittedly both black and white women suffer from a denial of independence and dignity. But no white woman knows the inhuman intentions of racial oppression. So black women in South Africa have an added burden caused by the effects of exploitation and oppression. Black women are the lowest paid work force in South Africa. In boom times they are hired at low wages and fired during recession periods. They form 70% of the unemployed community. They have to cook, wash, clean in their own homes after a very hard day's work. They form 60% of the church members, but are labelled as the weaker, subordinate, non-thinking people by their oppressed and exploited black men. Women can raise the funds but are not allowed in the church to decide how the funds are to be spent. With the rise of political violence in South Africa, more women have been raped by white troops in the townships and along the roadside than ever before. There are times when women fight side by side with their men in street wars against the army, yet they have no say in the decision-making body of the liberation struggle. Black women have to leave suckling babies behind and all their nurturing instincts would be wrenched from their bodies. Still they must go out to find work in a big city, very often only to become prostitutes.

The very beginnings of humankind are challenged. We live in the face of these demoralizing, dehumanizing conditions. It takes a superhuman being to just survive. And we, black women, have indeed survived. These dehumanizing situations are totally out of line with what God intended us to be at creation, for God gave dominion over all the earth to both male and female, with no specific color attached to it either. God used Moses to deliver the people of Israel. But it was Moses' mother who defied Pharoah's orders. Consequently she saved a child and eventually she saved the house of Israel. And isn't it also wonderful that God so designed the body of the woman that it would bear Christ the Liberator? Mary was not only concerned about a spiritual well-being when the angel of the Lord spoke to her. For instance, we read in Luke 1:51-53 in the Magnificat that Mary speaks about the political oppression of her people. Here she says that the mighty will be thrown from their throne.

Black Women's Experience and Black Theology

Thus the greatest event in the life of God's people was performed through an agent, a woman. Yet despite this, the rise of black theology did not initially consider the feminist aspect of *divine* liberation. However, I was very inspired by professor James Cone's acknowledgement of his own weaknesses when he was shaken into the reality of accepting how black theology, in essence, had to re-evaluate the legitimacy of its liberation claims. Specifically he realized that any form of liberation which does not address itself to the emancipation of the whole person should be seriously challenged for misrepresenting the concept of liberation. For no person can be free when part of that which gives you your humanity is in chains. A part of the wholeness of black womanness is also caught up in black theology and more specifically black feminist theology.

A very interesting thing happened in South Africa in 1956 when thousands of women marched to the Union buildings in Pretoria to protest against the passbooks. Most of them were Christian women from the pews in our churches, dominated by men. This example graphically shows the need for ongoing theological reflection on the nature of black women's faith in the liberation struggle. Therefore black feminist theology has to be an integral part of black theology. Granted, black theology is a particularization of our situation as black people in the societies in which we live. However, if black theology had been true to its self-assertion as part of a liberation theology of all humankind, black theology should have transformed into itself black feminist theology. It is sad that, as black oppressed women, we have had to put into the program of black theology, black feminist theology.

Our personal experience of God in our oppressed situation has given rise to the inevitable acceptance that God is on the side of the oppressed, the downtrodden, and the poor. We can read the book of Exodus. There God acts violently against those who perform degrading acts of oppression. God allows the Red Sea to close upon and down the military force of Pharoah. Whether we believe the Red Sea opened or closed is not the issue. But what is important is that the troops were washed away. They were violently destroyed.

Now I do not want to contend that men who oppress us women, and especially black men who oppress us black women, will be violently washed away. We love you and it makes the struggle more difficult. Yes, I do not wish you to be washed away. But I believe that male domination over female submission is not God ordained. We have to rectify this incorrect relation in the black community. Therefore we must use reconciliation together with repentance on the side of the oppressor and exploiter. Reconciliation together with repentance between black male and black female takes place in a just fashion. Each one of us has to recognize that one is not the enemy of the other. Rather we must focus on the real enemy of racist classism. In this situation, black women suffer the worst oppression and exploitation. Now God is no neutral God. Accordingly, it could then be claimed, and I do not want us to debate this issue, that God is supposed to be on the side of the black women. God is supposed to be a black woman. This might be so; it may not be so.

Black Feminist Theology's Origins

Above all, black women are prepared to accept God's granting dominion to all people over the earth. Black feminist theology in South Africa has only just begun, though it was written on the table long before people consciously got together to articulate the development of black feminist theology. Yet with the birth of the Johannesburg based Institute for Contextual Theology (ICT) toward the latter part of 1981, black feminist theology got off the ground deliberately. During this time, an exciting new era began to evolve in our communities. As the crisis errupted in our country, more women were taking up positions as equals with our men on the battlefield and at the drawing table. And at this point, we tried to sit down to really reflect on what was happening to us as oppressed women and to the black community as a whole.

But despite our involvement in the liberation struggle, women still had to be the slaves in our own homes. Black women, then, started getting together and added to the general thrust of black theology, a black feminist theology. However, it did not develop as a counter movement, but as an integral part of black theology. Unfortunately in 1985, black men at a black church leaders' ecumenical consultation held in South Africa laughed at the cries and distress of black feminist theologians. They laughed at what were real feelings of people. But nobody ever laughs at jokes about black people. Yet the cries and the anger of the women were real. The disappointment of realizing the insensitivity of other oppressed people was sad, but not disheartening. For a black woman is never disheartened. We cannot afford to loose heart.

For instance, when I was a student at the Federal Theological Seminary (supposedly one of the most progressive black oriented theological schools in South Africa), some new students would not participate in communion at the Lord's table when I served them. To add insult to injury, when my husband and I decided to have a baby and my tummy grew big with child, even those black men who initially received communion from me refused because I was no longer 'clean'. Thus we also find male seminary students, male church members, and male pastors acting extremely oppressive. But again, black women cannot afford to loose heart.

As the political crisis heightened in our country, the awareness of total liberation grew and women became more intensely aware of our position in the church and church related organizations. Specifically, we realized that our destiny as black women would be determined by how much we were prepared to fight a war for total liberation. In Luke 4, we read the famous words of Jesus saying: 'I have come to preach good news to the poor, to proclaim release to the captives... Sometimes Jesus' proclamation seems to be related only to men. But our experience tells us that the captives in South Africa (e.g., the poor, the blind, the oppressed) are women too, specifically black women. So Jesus died for all of us and rose for all of us.

Admittedly, black feminist theologians in South Africa are not highly 'qualified'. We are not all trained pastors. But black feminist theology is preached in the bushes of Nyanga in Cape Town. Black feminist theology is lived in the streets of downtrodden Soweto. It is lived in the shacks and preached in the shacks throughout South Africa. Black feminist theology is preached in the tents of forced removal townships. Black women in South Africa are involved at the grassroots developmental level of a theology from both our intellectual capacity as well as from our inner strength and from our gut feelings. For this reason, we find that black feminist theology does not differentiate itself from liberating political tendencies. They all work together; for the political oppression and exploitation gave birth to black feminist theology.

From an article in Zimbabwe, 'Consolidating A People's Power', we read how white colonial rule degraded black men and women in their own country. But women suffered greater humiliation than the men. Why? Because in the oppression of women, the chauvinistic elements of their own indigenous society aligned themselves with the chauvinistic elements in the white settler regime. Similarly, this is where our problem lies. For example, when the British and the Dutch decided to settle in South Africa, they decided to recognize local customary laws and to make them legally binding. These indigenous laws supported chauvinistic practices. Furthermore, the white settlers sent their men with all the assumptions of their own male dominated societies. Consequently, they did not give black women an opportunity to moderate the version of their position in society as given by men. And since that time, women have been considered legal minors. Customs that should have evolved naturally to meet the needs of a changing society were frozen by a law imposed upon the women. Likewise, the church as we have learned to experience it has evolved on this same creation of rule over people's lives and total lack of regard of human worth and dignity. The theology, then, reflected this pattern of master over servant.

However, with the emergence of black theology, this oppressive theology has been greatly challenged. Slowly but surely, and now in the 1980s, a theology challenging the inferior position of women has emerged. Black women are on the way to rediscover our tremendous power as black women in South Africa. Obviously there are still many who have not blossomed from their germinating period. But within the liberation movement and especially in black feminist theology, the ground has been tilled and now we shall work until the rains of justice shall fall from the heavens and breathe life into its once dormant receptors, heralding in a new way of awareness from the shackles of our oppressed bodies.

When white people came to South Africa, they had the bible and we had the land. But now we find that they have the land and we have the bible. This is why we have black theology. Thus black feminist theology does not intend to disqualify oppressed men from the saving grace of Jesus Christ. On the contrary, black women condemn white settlers for stealing the land from black men as well. Black feminist theology simply attempts to have black men view the struggle in a holistic way. Certainly all of the oppressed have to be set free to make the struggle a just struggle.

Indeed, we have the bible and the oppressors have the land. Yet it is from the soil of Africa that we blacks were called into a community with God. Because we have been called on the soil of Africa, that is where we have a relationship with God. But what kind of relationship can we have with God now that we have no soil? The soil has been taken from us. Even the wealth of the soil in the homelands, which are part of South Africa, is controlled by the racist regime. Moreover, this loss of our land for the bible affected both men and women. For example, men were forced to leave their homes to go to cities to find jobs and poverty, therefore, became a way of life. Women took control over the whole household and ran the affairs of the family. It was only when money ran short or when there was extreme illness that the women would go to the cities to join their husbands.

Yet nothing much has been written in the theologies of a believing people about such brave women. In contrast, books upon books have been written about great black men all depicting their struggle for survival. But women still have a greater struggle for survival. Black women today in South Africa know what it is like to nurse those injured in the streets as the struggle for liberation continues. We know what it is like to care for children not our own. The bible teaches us a gospel of caring and sharing. Sometimes, as black people who do not have, we find it difficult to preach the gospel of caring and sharing. Yet black women know what it is like to cry at the grave of some unknown comrade; not having personally known that person, but to have been involved with the spirit of that person for liberation. Black women in South Africa know what it is like to form support groups of victims of the system. In a word, through our own experiences, black women in South Africa are laying the foundation of a theology that makes God relevant to all people — a black feminist theology of liberation.

4

The Emergence of A Black Feminist Theology In the United States

Kelly D. Brown

In this essay, I have chosen to discuss the emergence of a black feminist theology in the United States. Like black theology in the United States and South Africa, black feminist theology has not emerged in academic institutions isolated from the wider black community. It too actually began with a social movement. Indeed, black feminist theology can trace its roots back to the 1960s civil rights and black consciousness movements.

Civil Rights and Black Consciousness

During the 1960s black protest movements, black women joined black men in marching, sitting-in, going to jail, being beaten and risking their lives all for the sake of black freedom. In some instances black women were the leaders of black protests and the initiators of civil rights organizations. For example, it was Ella Baker who asked Martin Luther King, Jr. why there was no organized follow-up to the 1956-57 Montgomery bus boycott, thereby setting in motion the founding of the Southern Christian Leadership Conference (SCLC). It was also Ella Baker who recognized the potential of a coordinated student movement and, thus, called college students from across the country to a conference at Shaw University (Raleigh, North Carolina) in April, 1960. As a result of this conference, the Student Nonviolent Coordinating Committee (SNCC) was formed. In addition, it was Gloria Richardson who led the 1962 Cambridge Maryland Movement, the first contemporary 'grass-roots' movement against the segregation of public accommodations to take place outside of the Southern United States. And certainly without the efforts and courage of Fannie Lou Hamer, the Mississippi Freedom Democratic Party would have never been formed. It was she who led the delegates from this group to the 1964 Atlantic City Democratic Convention, where under her leadership they mounted a campaign to be seated as the official delegation from Mississippi. Beyond the more public figures like Baker, Richardson or Hamer, there were also the Joann Robinsons, Diane Nashs, Unita Blackwells, Annie Mae Kings, Ruby Doris Smiths, Emma Jenkins, and scores of other black women who made significant contributions to the civil rights and black consciousness movements.

Yet, regardless of the pivotal roles which they played, black women were never accorded the same treatment or respect as their black male colleagues. Often, the very men with whom they worked made it clear to them that black women would have no visible leadership in the various civil rights organizations, and that all final decision-making powers belonged to men not women. Dorothy Cotton, the highest ranking woman in SCLC, observed a definite 'woman's place' in the organization. Ella Baker has supported Cotton's observations by acknowledging the impossibility of a leadership role for her in SCLC during the 1960s, primarily because she was a woman. Perhaps the statement which has been used most often to characterize black male attitudes within the civil rights and black consciousness organizations was one made in 1968 by SNCC chairperson Stokely Carmichael. In response to a grievance paper presented by the women of SNCC, Carmichael said, 'The only position for women is prone'.

Black Women's Consciousness

In part, as a result of black women recognizing the contradiction of being a part of freedom fighting organizations which actively discriminated against them and as black men continued to display blatant sexist attitudes and behaviors, a black feminist consciousness emerged. Black women began to articulate the unique oppression connected to being *both* black and woman. They began to realize that to be black and woman in the United States too often means being unemployed in a disproportionate percentage to the rest of the population. In other words, black women have indeed been the 'last hired and the first fired'. In addition, if a black woman is employed, it more than likely means she is earning substandard wages and, moreover, raising children alone on these meager wages. It should be noted that still today, according to the 1980 United States Census, 70 percent of all black families that fall below the poverty line are headed by a woman.

Again, a black feminist consciousness in the United States emerged as black women began to recognize and articulate their unique oppression. As they did this they began to search their past and lift up the words and works of other black women who, in their own times, articulated the special burdens attached to black womanhood. The words of women like Harlem Renaissance writer Zora Neale Hurston helped black women to understand the complexity of their situation. Through a fictional character, Hurston described the black woman's plight in the United States this way:

> Honey, de white man is de ruler of everything as fur as Ah been able tuh find out. Maybe it's some place way off in de ocean where de black man is in power, but we don't know nothin' but what we see. So de white man throw down de load and tell de nigger man tuh pick it up. He pick it up because he have to, but he don't tote it. He hand it to his womenfolks. De nigger woman is de mule uh de world so fur as Ah can see.

The work which perhaps marks the beginning of a contemporary black woman's consciousness in the United States is the 1970 anthology edited by Toni Cade, *The Black Woman*. This anthology contains a series of essays by black women, from full-time mothers to college professors, in which they discuss their experience as black women and search for ways in which to gain their freedom without becoming alienated from the black community as a whole — that is, from their black men.

Black Feminist Theology

Now, as a part of this developing consciousness of what it means to be black and woman, a black feminist theology has emerged. Black women began to recognize that it was not just within secular organizations and within the black community in general that they were being discriminated against. They also realized their marginal status within the black church.

If the experience of being black and woman can in general be described as a 'double jeopardy', black churchwoman Theressa Hoover described the experience of black women in the church as a 'triple jeopardy'. Black women, like Hoover, have addressed the contradiction involved in a church (e.g., the black church) which emerged in a protest against oppression and which espouses a belief in a Jesus Christ who is liberator of those who are oppressed, yet continually oppresses its own members. Black women have questioned why black church leadership is not reflective of the fact that 75 percent of the black congregations are female.

As black women began to critique the black church, the critique extended also to the theology which emerged from that church, that is, the black theology of liberation. Jacquelyn Grant provided the earliest critique of black theology in her 1979 article, 'Black Theology and the Black Woman'. In this article she accused black theologians of not seriously addressing the issue of sexism. And in fact, as black theologians ignored the experiences of black women, they actually rendered black women 'invisible' within their theologies. Grant ended her 1979 assessment of black theology by charging that with black women representing more than 50 percent of the black community and more than 70 percent of the black church, no 'authentic theology of liberation (can) arise out of these communities without specifically addressing the liberation of women in both places'. Finally, Grant challenged black women to continue to name their experience of oppression and 'to keep the issue of sexism 'going' in the Black community, in the Black Church, and in Black Theology until it has been eliminated'.

Black Feminist Theology Today

This brings us to the current status of a black feminist theology within the United States. For indeed, black women have responded to Grant's challenge to keep the issue of sexism going.

What black women are currently doing in theology can be described as a threefold task. The first is the critical task. Black women are in the process of critiquing those theologies which, by their very name, suggest that they should at least include the experiences of black women. Specifically, black women are critiquing black and feminist theologies in the United States.

Jacquelyn Grant, for instance, provided an extended analysis of feminist theology in her doctoral dissertation, *The Development and Limitation of Feminist Christologies: Toward An Engagement of White and Black Women's Religious Experiences.* In this work she explored the central issues of white feminist theologians as they tried to articulate Jesus Christ's significance for women. In her examination, she concludes that feminist theology ignores black women's faith experiences; therefore what white feminists call women's concerns about Jesus Christ are not reflective of black women's concerns.

Delores Williams has put the question sharply in relation to white feminist theology. She has challenged white feminists to clearly name the experience of oppression which they describe, (e.g., their theological and christological perspectives) as those of white women, not women in general. Furthermore, I am currently engaged in a critique of black theology where I am looking at its significance to and representation of black women's faith.

Now, as this conference is a dialogue on black theologians in the United States and South Africa, let me pause a moment and share with you one aspect of what I am finding as I critically examine US black theology.

With a few exceptions, black theologians have continued to ignore the unique oppression of black women within the black church and community. In essence, they have not made the elimination of sexism central to their liberation concerns. Regardless of their own theological commitment to the God of the Exodus and of their recognition that any form of oppression goes against the love and justice of God, black theologians have not challenged black male ministers and church officials as they refuse ordination and leadership positions to black women. Although black theologians, and even black ministers, can readily see the injustice in South Africa as the vast black majority is denied any political leadership, and even though they protest vigorously against the South African system which does not allow black people to have some say over their own destiny, black theologians and ministers do not seem to recognize a similar situation of oppression within their own backyard. Again, 75 percent of our black church congregations are composed of women, yet women are consistently denied leadership roles. Black women give the money to the church, but have no voice in how that money is to be spent. Black women financially build and secure the pulpits, but are not allowed in them. So, why is it that black male theologians and ministers can declare: 'None of us are free until all of us are free', connecting to the struggles against apartheid while ignoring the lack of freedom within their own church and community?

In part, the answer to this is found in the fact that it is always harder to critique the oppression within one's own backyard – especially if one is receiving benefits from it. In this regard, just as the black majority of South Africa cannot expect the white minority to eagerly dismantle the system of apartheid which allows them control and power, black women cannot expect black male ministers and theologians to eagerly critique and dismantle the 'ole boy' system of the black church which gives black men control and power. Instead, black feminist theologians must be the ones to empower black women to call the oppressive demon of sexism by name in the black church and community. In so doing, black women must struggle against this demon so that the black church can become whole and, thus, more accurately represent in its ministry and leadership the God of the Exodus who is neither male nor female.

In essence, as I and other black feminist theologians critically evaluate feminist and black liberation theologies' exclusion of black women's experiences, we are discovering their (that is, black and feminist theologies') inadequate representation of what it means today for God and hence Jesus Christ to be a liberator of the oppressed. Our findings continue to affirm Grant's earlier observation that any 'authentic theology of liberation', arising specifically within the black community, must address the unique oppression of black women.

This leads us to the remaining two tasks of black women as they do theology. These tasks are the explorative and constructive tasks. Black women are exploring the lives, fictional and non-fictional writings, prayers as well as their own personal experiences, in an effort to understand the meaning of God and Jesus Christ for black women. In this regard, Grant is in the process of exploring what it means for a black woman like Sojourner Truth to exclaim that as she bears the burdens of black womanhood, none but Jesus hears. At the same time, Delores Williams is searching for ways to help black women view Jesus as not just one who hears about their struggles, pains and oppression, but also as one who actively participates in trying to liberate them from those struggles, pains and oppression. Black feminist ethicist Katie Cannon has been exploring the works of Zora Neale Hurston in search of a constructive ethic for black women. Other black women, like Evelyn Brooks and Cheryl Gilkes, have been exploring the histories of black women in the Black Baptist and Pentecostal churches in an effort to reveal what has been a continuing presence of a prophetic black feminist voice within a traditionally male institution.

Black women are doing this exploratory work in order to fully understand what the God who liberated the Hebrew children from Egyptian bondage and delivered Jesus from Pilate's cross has to say to black women enslaved by the cross of racism, sexism and poverty. And, what are they finding? What will a black feminist theology say about God and Jesus Christ so that the Gospel will speak to the particularity of the oppressed and also have some universal significance? At this point, let me share again some ideas from my own efforts to develop a systematic understanding of Jesus Christ which is more reflective of black women's experiences.

First of all, as part of my constructive task, I am discovering how black churchwomen — like black churchmen — rarely make a distinction between God and Jesus. Jesus is God, that is why black church people can sing:

> He's King of Kings and Lord of Lord,
> Jesus Christ, the first and the last
> No man works like him.

Such a confession of Jesus as Lord, as God, as the Christ, was an affirmation by black slaves that the God of their slave masters was not the real God. God was not the One who ordained and supported their slavery. Instead, God was the One who came through Jesus Christ as friend and liberator of the oppressed. Therefore, God was there to sustain them as they suffered and to free them from their bondage. In short, because black Christians know Jesus, through scripture and in their own lives, they knew (contrary to what whites might say) God was for them and not against them.

In this regard, the confession of Jesus as the Christ is an affirmation of God's commitment to the poor and oppressed. It is a confession born not out of the tradition of Nicea and Chalcedon, but out of the history of slavery. It is a confession made not in an effort to show the uniqueness of Jesus or as an attempt to understand the mystery of the incarnation. Instead, it is made in an effort to affirm the God of liberation, not of slavery. Such a confession of Jesus as the Christ is what allows a black woman like Sojourner Truth to say, 'I cried out with my mother's grief, none but Jesus heard me', or black women to sing, 'He is the lily of the Valley and the bright and morning star'.

Moreover, this confession, its history and its meaning, presents at least a twofold challenge to the black church. First, it reminds the black church that its history of understanding the power of Jesus Christ's presence in black lives is not the same as the white church's history. The questions black Christians have asked concerning the significance of God's incarnation in Jesus are not the same as those of white Christians. Consequently, neither are their answers. Therefore, the black church is challenged to be faithful to its own history, its own questions and its answers and, thus, develop its own creed which expresses the meaning of God and Jesus Christ for black Christians, as opposed to blindly adopting the Nicene creed.

Secondly, the black church's confession of Jesus as the Christ, and thus God as liberator, should act as a constant challenge to the black church to live according to that which it confesses. In other words, the black church is challenged by its own confession of faith to eliminate any structure, system or pattern of behavior which is not commensurate with a church that proclaims the liberating God as its center.

On the other hand, whereas recognizing Jesus as the Christ has been liberating for black men and women, it has also contributed to black women's oppression. Specifically, Jesus' maleness often has been used to exclude black women from the ordained ministry. Many black ministers have exclaimed against women's ordination because the model for the ordained ministry is Jesus, who is male.

Furthermore, we must ask the following question. As long as Christ is so tied to the historical Jesus, will it ever be possible for black women to see the possibilities of Christ within themselves and themselves in Christ, or to move from an understanding of Christ as one who not only hears their pain but also acts to eliminate it? In essence, will it ever be possible for black women to conceive of Christ or even God as anything but male? The urgency of this problem recently became clear to me when a black woman asked me not to refer to God as she. 'It just doesn't sound right,' the black woman said.

Again, for black women, confessing Jesus as the Christ has been both liberating and oppressive. Therefore, a black feminist theology must reflect this history in what it says about the meaning of Jesus Christ. In doing this, I think it must articulate the meaning of Jesus Christ by emphasizing his *actions* in human history, not his biological characteristics. One must draw attention to the meaning of his death and resurrection rather than his biological particularities of Jewishness and maleness. Consequently, the symbols we use to express Jesus' significance for us today must point not toward a biological feature or characteristic, but toward the activity of Jesus as the liberator.

Even more, a black feminist theology must challenge black Christians by asking if confessing Jesus as the Christ necessarily eliminates other examples or incarnations of God's presence in human history? A black feminist theology must affirm that for black Christians, Jesus is the Christ. It is He who acts as the ultimate witness to God's revelation on the side of the poor and oppressed. But he is not the only witness. Jesus, through his liberating activity, should act as a guide for black Christians to see other incarnations of God in the world. In this way, the possibility is opened for black women to see Christ in themselves and themselves in Christ, as well as for black Christians to dialogue and unite with other oppressed peoples who do not confess Jesus as the Christ.

Now, what does all this mean in our dialogue with black South African theology? First, a black South African theology can learn from the mistakes and limitations of black theology in the US. As black theologians in South Africa are still in the process of developing a systematic understanding of what it means for God and Jesus Christ to be liberator in their context of oppression, they should recognize the necessity to speak of oppression in a holistic manner that reflects the lives of both men and women. Instead of following US black theologians' lead and ignoring half of their population, and thus creating theologies of liberation that inadequately represent Jesus' liberating presence in human history, black theologians of South Africa – men and women – should dialogue and do theology together.

Indeed, as we have seen from the response to black theology in the US, it is not enough for black male theologians to casually mention the need to eliminate gender oppression and then go on with the rest of their theological agenda. Instead, their theological agendas must maintain as central a concern to eliminate any form of oppression which affects God's people. More specifically, race, class and gender oppression must always be held together at the very least. Thus, women's issues should not be viewed as an afterthought to one's theology or an addendum to a conference; instead they should be integral to one's liberating concerns.

On the other hand, given the fact that our own particular social political situations can reveal aspects of God's revelation in human history that other situations do not reveal, black women in South Africa and the United States must continue to do theology for themselves, thus expressing the meaning of God and Jesus Christ in their lives. Moreover, given the fact that our situations of oppression bear similarities, black women in the US and South Africa should remain in consistent conversation, learning from and sharing with each other. Though black American women are an oppressed majority within an oppressed minority and black South African women are an oppressed majority within an oppressed majority, nevertheless we are both searching for ways to voice our own concerns without sacrificing the concerns of our wider community. We are both fighting for the freedom to represent the ministry of Jesus Christ in our churches. As put best by Zora Neale Hurston, we are both 'the mule of the world'. Therefore, as we each develop our black feminist theologies of liberation, we should remember that the universality of Jesus Christ's message means our freedom signifies nothing apart from the freedom of our sisters across the water.

5

'Present Socio-Political-Economic Movements for Change'

Cornel West

I would like to cast my presentation at three levels. The first has to do with the normative level — what kinds of values and norms emanate from the Christian tradition and what kind of resources can we cull from that tradition, a tradition (as in South Africa and other places) that has been misused and distorted. In fact given this tradition, it takes tremendous audacity to be a Christian these days, especially in South Africa. What kind of demands, requirements, obligations, and duties flow therefrom?

The second level, the crucial level, deals with socio-economic analysis and with concrete institutional embodiments and the concrete social practices that flow from a particular socio-economic analysis. And the last level is that of action and praxis; that is to say, what kind of engagement can be enacted in light of the socio-economic analysis and based on the norms and values put forth from the Christian tradition?

The Normative Level

To be a progressive and prophetic Christian in the United States and South Africa, one has to speak to the personal level. Indeed, it has to do with issues of integrity, character and discipline. To be a Christian means to exemplify what one espouses. It is precisely a personal issue of integrity because it is quite easy to talk and engage in rhetoric without seriously coming to terms with what one espouses. This is especially true in the United States where commitment becomes a kind of commodity. Thus commitment-talk becomes fashionable. In contrast, this is not the case in South Africa where commitment means ultimately contemplating the loss of one's life.

Moreover, we have to talk seriously about what kind of very profound levels of risk and sacrifice are necessary. Specifically, we speak of courage, the basic act of placing the needs of others over and beyond that of oneself. Oftentimes, especially in prophetic discourse, we tend to skip over this moment. Rather, we need to particularly highlight it given the situation of our brothers and sisters in South Africa. Because they have to deal with it every day. We in the United States tend to hold personal sacrifice at arms' length because we do not have the repressive state apparatus staring us in the face as directly and immediately as do the brothers and sisters in apartheid South Africa.

Thus the issue of courage and sacrifice challenges our Christian faith. What does it mean to be a Christian in a context in which class, racial and gender contradictions (e.g., social institutional sins) are so intense, overwhelming and pervasive that it might require giving up one's life? To attempt an answer to such a profound personal and existential dilemma, we turn to the normative level. Out of the Christian tradition, I would like to emphasize three notions, norms or values.

The first is the notion of the *imago dei*, a very traditional notion: to be made in the image of God; to spotlight the sanctity and the dignity of individuals. All individuals are unique and made in God's image and thereby warrant a certain kind of treatment. This is very important because it relates to the universalism and the egalitarianism of the Christian gospel. I would suggest that '*imago dei*', in the present situation, has subversive implications. It has revolutionary implications. Though it sounds like a simple theological point, it, in fact, diametrically opposes the hierarchical structures that we see shot through societies such as the United States and South Africa.

The second notion is 'fallenness'. Fallenness does not have a popular status because it deals with the whole classical formulations of sin. As Christians, however, we should take very seriously sin on the personal and institutional levels. In fact, a serious grappling with sin allows me to arrive at very radical democratic values. For example, the abuse of power is inherent in excessive power; absolute power corrupts absolutely. Therefore, we need accountability mechanisms to thwart such a sin. We need radical democratic institutions to account for all forms of power and to maintain checks and balances; not simply in the political sphere, but in the economic and the cultural also.

'Kingdom-talk' or the coming of the Kingdom, the last notion, responds to what I consider to be the most fundamental issue in talking about South Africa and the United States. For Christians, that is the problem of evil; how does one respond to and resist the forms of evil, institutional evil especially. Thus Kingdom-talk provides a means of, on the one hand, sustaining some sense of meaning in a meaningless situation. And most important, on the other hand, it allows one to undergo empowerment in a situation in which one feels relatively powerless.

Kingdom-talk offers, then, a way by which the in-breaking of the Kingdom into the present sustains hope for those undergoing a struggle against overwhelming odds, and offers a source of empowerment in a situation in which the power seems to reside on the surface among those elites, among the ruling classes who deploy the most repressive terroristic means of regulating the population.

In summary, three notions occupy the normative level — the *imago dei*, fallenness, and the Kingdom's coming.

The Level of Social Analysis

I would like to spend much more time on the second level, the level of social analysis. I cannot stress enough how important social analysis is in understanding the operations of the multi-level, multi-dimensional operations of power; that is, how one understands wealth, prestige, status, influence and how these circulate in a particular society. Indeed, I would go so far as to argue that most of the battles within the Christian tradition these days have to do with battles over social analysis. For instance, all Christians today seem to be for freedom, equality, and democracy. Yes, but the question is how do you interpret these claims; what is the analytical content and substance of these assertions? The analytical content and substance are supplied by one's social analysis. As Christians, we wish to employ social analysis from the vantage point of society's victims, from the vantagepoint of those who suffer, from the vantagepoint of the Cross, the christocentric perspective. Therefore the types of social analyses we would deploy not only attempt to interpret the world but also attempt to isolate potentialities for ultimate realization in struggle.

Accordingly, we must note that our overall discursive context is a battle. Here is one of the few places I agree with John Calvin: human history is in fact a battleground for struggle, contestation, conflict, and resistance. The question is not only on what side are you but also how you understand the side that you are on such that you can ultimately triumph. The aim is to win, to expand the scope of democracy, to expand the scope of individuals who have a status of sanctity and dignity. In this sense, social analysis is a weapon, a tool, an instrument for struggle. This is very important because a lot of our secular comrades, especially on the left, tend to make social analysis and tools of social analysis themselves fetishes and idols. Whereas, for Christians, social analyses serve simply as tools and instruments.

Social and historical analyses aid us in historically situating and locating a people at a particular moment. Where is the struggle in South Africa at this particular moment? Where is the struggle in the United States at this particular moment? In response, I would like to begin with the 'Europeanization of the world'. In particular, we live at the end of the age of Europe which began roughly in 1492 and ended in 1945. And, of course, post-1945 World War II is the start of the American century. The century only lasted for 28 years, from 1945 to 1973. But, nonetheless, post-World War II US ascendancy marked the beginning of an American century. The 'Europeanization of the world' and the American century serve as historical backdrops in our comprehending the tremendous resurgence of insurgency and resistance in the United States (principally black led in the 1950s with Martin Luther King, Jr.) and, of course, the tremendous insurgency in South Africa post-World War II (symbolically best represented by the June 16th Soweto Student Rebellion).

What exactly do I mean by the 'Europeanization of the world'? I designate particular institutional life denying forces with a global and international scope. More specifically, I would characterize them as exploitation, domination, repression, and subjugation. Oftentimes, we utilize these terms in an interchangeable manner. But I suggest that they are not identical and synonymous at all. True, they inseparably connect in the concrete world in which we live. Yet for analytical purposes, we can distinguish them. Here our social and historical analyses provide a means to engage these four institutional forms of evil which confront Americans and South Africans as children of God struggling for freedom and liberation.

Economic Exploitation

The first, economic exploitation, deals with the emergence of the capitalist mode of production. Here marxist analysis becomes indispensible (as we shall see, I think, it is ultimately inadequate; but it is indispensible). Marxist analysis acts as one of the essential components in a Christian understanding of institutional forms of evil. In other words, we cannot understand the Europeanization of the world without understanding the emergence of the capitalist mode of production and the impact that it has had on victims in the world, specifically for our purposes, on people of African descent. The capitalist mode of production attempts to extend its scope around the globe. A graphic example: in 1834, European powers owned 35% of the land on the globe. By 1918, they controlled 87% of the land on the globe.

But what do we mean by the capitalist mode of production? This historically constituted mode of production signifies classes being formed in social relations of production. It signifies a minority owning the land and the instruments of production and forcing the majority to work, to sell its labor power, and to sell its time and energy and skills to those who own that land and instruments of production. Thus capital, in this sense, is not mere money or revenue. It is a *social* relation concerned with relative powerlessness. At this juncture, we discover a major misunderstanding by the majority of Americans. Even as they live lives of prosperity, most Americans live lives of powerlessness.

Consequently, living in a capitalist society by definition suggests a life of material insecurity, precisely because you have no control over the conditions of your work place. For example, small farmers in rural Oklahoma believed they lived lives of prosperity until the structural shift in capitalism threw them onto the anarchic market. We could say the same thing about workers in Norwood, Ohio who were informed that General Motors planned to close. Of course we could say the same thing about the large numbers of unemployed persons in South Africa whom the ruling class utilizes as a reserve labor army to ensure low wages and also to militaristically control the South African labor force.

Hence a marxist analysis of the capitalist mode of production proves indispensible in determining which movements we will join and in comprehending the maldistribution of wealth in South Africa and the United States. The maldistribution of wealth supercedes the common sense notion of how many swimming pools and big houses one owns (i.e., in white Johannesburg). Yes, that is one manifestation. But my analysis of wealth speaks to the fundamental structural impediments and constraints for property and holdings. Part of the problem, especially in the United States, lies with our definition of wealth. We tend to think of income rather than holdings, earnings rather than property holdings. In fact most of the economic data one finds pinpoint how much money people make. But that is not wealth. Wealth involves ownership. Even the American middle class does not own much. They might have credit cards that allow a certain lifestyle, but they do not own much. The picture focuses more clearly when we turn to South Africa. But we should not think that the US has a more equitable or egalitarian distribution of wealth. On the contrary, the US capitalist pie is so large that a number of persons are able to share it and call themselves middleclass when they are actually workers, exploited by the capitalist system.

Again, a social analysis of capitalist economic exploitation is crucial. Here we must guard against classifying exploitation as simply a moral term. Marx's *Kapital* makes a great contribution in clarifying this when his work defines exploitation as a relation that results in relative powerlessness. Far from a mere finger pointing moral critique, exploitation involves an analytic interpretation of the structural constraints of distributing wealth that results in a small number of people monopolizing tremendous wealth and the majority of persons having little wealth at all.

State Repression

The second level of the Europeanization of the world deals with state repression. The people of African descent know state repression quite well. For instance, black people in the southern USA had to undergo crypto-fascist institutionalized terrorism for over 250 years; lynching being one of the most salient examples of institutionalized terrorism. Thus state repression represents the deployment of the repressive state apparatus in order to control persons. It links principally to the military, to the army, to the prisons, to the police, etc. Though state repression is inseparable from economic exploitation, it is not the same thing. It maintains its own relative autonomy. However ultimately, the ruling elites in the economic sphere of society dictate to the state. In this instance, Michael Foucaux's works help us to come to terms with forms of state repression: surveillance, torture, and disciplinary control.

Bureaucratic Domination

'Bureaucratic domination', the third level of the Europeanization of the world, is very important because it permeates both capitalist modes of production as well as state repressive apparatuses.

Furthermore, because they are hierarchical, bureaucracies entail the means for rhetorics of submission and subordination. (At the same time, we should always note the historically determined nature of all bureaucracies. In other words, they do not have to contain their present hierarchical state.) Thus today's bureaucracies construct various ways to check people's power. Not only do political movements become bureaucratized themselves, but they also suffer from bourgeois bureaucracies that diffuse and dilute their energies in an attempt to suck off the people's leadership and incorporate that leadership into these intentionally, lethargic bourgeois institutions. These bureaucracies claim efficiency; that was the ideological justification for modern forms of bureaucracy that Max Weber analyzed. But in reality, we know that the basic aim of bureaucracy is self-perpetuation. Again, they have their own relative autonomy.

So far we have touched upon economic exploitation and its relation to profit maximization, the political sphere (on the state) and its relation to controlling the instrumentalities of violence (as well as the institutions of public administration), and bureaucratic domination and its relation to self-perpetuity.

Subjugation

We now come to 'subjugation', the final manifestation of the Europeanization of the world. Subjugation concerns racism (so fundamental in both histories of the USA and South Africa), sexism, homophobia, etc. Subjugation concerns the social and historical construction of particular identities and subjectivities; which is to say issues of self-perception or self-image or, what Marcus Garvey called, 'identity'. This plays a crucial role in grasping various socio-political movements because the way in which you view yourself is one of the means by which you acquire empowerment.

For instance in American history, the identity issue pervades in the construction of the Negro subject as opposed to black subjects, African subjects as opposed to Afro-American subjects. Garvey understood the significance of identity. It is no accident that he led the largest mass movement in the United States. Indeed, the cultural resources and the sense of cultural agency (e.g., identity) are inseparable from the political agency. How you conceive yourself is inseparable from what you perceive yourself doing politically. Therefore, to the degree that you understand yourself as degraded, inferior, and subordinate precludes and forecloses political possibilities for how you will act. Similarly, how you view yourself as not only a child of God but also as an African with a proud heritage, past, and history, affects how you think about the future and how you act in the present.

In summary, all four examples of institutional evil are part and parcel of the appropriate social analysis needed by Christians. The first level of evil principally relates to Marx (e.g., economic exploitation). The second level principally relates to Foucaux (e.g., state repression). The third principally relates to Weber (e.g., bureaucratism). And the fourth relates to Garvey and Malcolm X (e.g., anti-racist and anti-sexist subjugation). All four go hand-in-hand.

The Praxis Level

In dealing with the 'present socio-political-economic movements for change', so far we have explored the normative and social analysis levels. We now reach the final section, the level of praxis.

Aristotle argued that the conclusion of a practical syllogism was not a resolution but an action. I would want to argue that it is the same in any analysis for Christians. More specifically, if one does not ultimately talk about engaging in action and praxis, then one's talk is academic; it is simply discursive as opposed to political action. Thus the question becomes: in what possible actions and potential practices can one engage? Of course the contexts of the United States and South Africa are, on the one hand, inseparable, and, on the other, different.

First a look at South Africa. In that country, we see those movements that are against economic exploitation and therefore are radically anti-capitalist. We see those movements that are against state repression and thereby are anti-repressive state apparatus, that are in fact anti-hierarchical. And therefore, they are concerned about democratizing the bureaucratic institutions. Lastly, we see those movements that are fundamentally anti-subjugation which means that they are anti-racist and anti-sexist.

What kinds of movements does one then attempt to put forward? A lot depends on the weight placed on each of the four institutional evils elaborated above. In other words, if one views capitalist economic exploitation at the center of evil, then one's political movement will primarily focus on economic exploitation. However, if one surmises identity as the principal evil, then one's energies will stress the importance of the African identity in a white dominated world. Here issues of black consciousness and black positive identity will come to the center.

In my judgement, one encounters one of the most salutary developments in South Africa when one observes most resistance movements interweaving all four kinds of institutional evils in their analysis. Whether one speaks of the Azanian Peoples' Organization (AZAPO) or the United Democratic Front (UDF), all posit a holistic analysis against evil.

Given the necessity for an integrated approach to institutional evils, what should be the proper Christian response to economic exploitation, state repression, bureaucratic domination, and racist (and sexist) subjugation? I would want to argue for three basic options for South Africa. First, one could pursue armed struggle and guerrilla warfare. Second, one could undertake various kinds of community actions characterized by mobilizing and organizing black and progressive whites. Finally, there exists the church's attempt to not play a 'third role'. I like the *Kairos Document's* critique of the church's false belief in its ability to stand above the fray and mediate as if the very conflict itself has not already penetrated and divided the church. No, the church has to take a stand. It has to choose in such a way that it preserves its Christian identity; yet that Christian identity itself does not become a fetish. On the one hand, Christians must uphold their Christian identity while entering social movements and political organizations. On the other hand, a Christian should not become so preoccupied with one's Christian self that it separates you from the social struggle.

Armed Struggle

What potentialities exist for the first option of armed struggle and guerrilla warfare? First, we should acknowledge the current existence of armed struggle. But it is weak and feeble given the situation of the strength of the South Africa state. Nevertheless, guerrilla warfare tragically exemplifies a symptom of just how deep the evil is. Indeed, Christians who wish to speak of a just war or just rebellion or just revolution would have to have a very deep doctrine of evil and sin and how to combat such sin.

Second, I think highly of the pacifist tradition in Christendom. I do not agree with it; I am not persuaded by it. But I think it is respectful. I do not think Christian pacifists will ever have the kind of impact on history that many of them would purport to have. Yet I respect their views. So when I hear archbishop Tutu or Allan Boesak and many others argue for non-violence, I respect them. Furthermore, without doubt, one should, on principled ground, attempt to exercise and realize all forms of non-violent resistance before one even entertains the discussion of violent resistance and armed struggle. Then we have to look at the history of a country and see what possibilities have there been for non-violent resistance and what impact non-violent resistance has had. If we, in fact, discover that non-violent resistance in its most noble form has been crushed mercilessly by the rulers, then it raises the possibility of forced engagement in armed struggle. Indeed, this is no way alien to the Christian tradition. For instance, the Christian ruling class of the United States claims that the American Revolutionary War, the Civil War, World War I, World War II, the Korean War, and the Vietnam War were all necessary and Christian. Yet, when black folk begin to think of armed struggle, the white ruling elite responds: 'well, we've got some complex problems we've got to come to terms with before we even entertain the possibility of armed self-defense'. It is this type of intellectual arrogance (and racism) that one has to resist.

But, on the other hand, one should never view armed struggle as a plaything. One should not romanticize or idealize it at all. On the contrary, one should carefully and thoroughly think through whether it can have the impact and effectiveness that one desires. Specifically for South Africa, that means weighing relations with neighboring countries; whether there will be space and support from them.

In my estimation, if the majority of South Africans reach the conclusion that all forms of non-violent resistance have been called into question (that, in fact, the current civil war requires self-defensive violent resistance as well as ultimate transformative violent resistance), then it is incumbent upon Christians in the First World to not only support that kind of activity but to also provide understanding of it to other people in the First World. We witnessed this process in the 1960s as Africa underwent decolonization. Likewise this last bastion of Afrikaner colonization will require the same kind of solidarity and support from Christians and people of goodwill as those in the 1960s did for Ghana, Kenya, and other African nations.

However, South Africa, it seems to me, is in many ways still far removed from a situation in which effective armed struggle and guerrilla warfare can be waged. It might, indeed, be on the agenda in the next 15 or 20 years. But today, a variety of different obstacles impede violent resistance: such as the destabilization of neighboring African countries by the South African government; and the role the United States could play both covertly and explicitly in its support for the apartheid state against such resistance.

Mobilization and Organization

Because armed struggle ultimately depends upon how well one relates to the masses of people, we next move to mobilization and organization. One cannot simply emerge and commence fighting. For instance, I think the tremendous courage and heroism that we see in South Africa among the young folk (particularly since their 1984 student revolt) has to do with a political impatience. But political impatience differs from thoroughly thought-out strategy and tactics, thoroughly thought out mobilization and organization. You need that subversive energy of the youth and students if you are going to have strategy and tactics. But sheer political impatience, in and of itself, can result in becoming mere cannon fodder for the repressive state apparatus in South Africa.

Therefore the question becomes organizing and mobilization which relates to consciousness. By consciousness, I am suggesting orientation and direction and convincing persons regarding credible alternatives. People will not engage in a revolutionary leap of faith until they, on the one hand, see such acts of valor and courage manifest (which has been the case in South Africa) and, on the other hand, are convinced of the lack of other credible alternatives. There is still a deep problem of conscientizing the masses in South Africa, it seems to me. Black South Africans do not comprise a monolithic or homogenous block.

Consequently, in that context one has to develop religious and ideological contestation. And the organizing and mobilizing would target this ongoing conscientization process: at the cultural level of identity, African heritage, overcoming the racist self-perception; at the level of the economic sphere in terms of what particular form does capitalism take in South Africa in exploiting the majority of the population; and in the political sphere in terms of rule of law. 'Rule of law' sounds like liberalism; but liberalism at its best is an indispensible element in any socialist vision or any egalitarian vision. Why? Because liberalism connotes equal status before the law, one-person-one-vote, which in South Africa today is subversive. The protection of rights and liberties (e.g., liberalism) remains basic.

In summary, conscientization must proceed in the political, economic and cultural spheres. And Christian churches have the obligation to participate in that kind of concientization, given the previously mentioned resources of *imago dei*, made equal in the image of God; of fallenness and therefore the need for accountability structures and radical democratic mechanisms; and of this coming Kingdom or Kingdom-talk, this unquenchable quest for freedom.

The Christian Church

I would like to end by noting the role of Christian churches. In a sense, we in the United States need the energies of the masses of South Africa. We in the United States currently suffer a profound demoralization. The pacification of our communities by drugs and alcohol, by the cultural industry of television and radio, by music

However, all of us are caught in addiction and stimulation of some sort. But the black and brown communities receive concentrations of the more deadly, demonic forms. Therefore demoralization and pacification set in. As a result, it makes it very difficult for leaders to emerge, to be courageous. To be courageous, one has to step out by oneself. Today that is much more difficult than it was in the 1960s when more people were stepping out alongside you. Again, in that sense, this leadership vacuum is something that we black folk in the United States, we Africans in the United States have to take very seriously and to learn from and be inspired by South Africans. In particular, we can learn from the progressive stand taken by Christians who support the *Kairos Document*. Clearly, now is the time for the church's role to be prophetic, persuasive and pacesetting; that is, in the interests of the poor against perpetrators of exploitation, domination, repression, and subjugation.

6

Present Socio-Political-Economic Movements for Change

Simon S. Maimela

In this chapter I will refer to a number of movements which are pressing for change in South Africa. Some of these movements need to be viewed against the background of the 1976 Soweto Student Rebellion in South Africa.[1] That revolt forced the government of South Africa and its supporters to go back to the drawing board in order to draft a new blueprint to suppess the ensuing resistance movement in the country.

The Government's Maneuvering

In response to the Student Revolt in 1976, the apartheid government took some action, for it realized that its days were numbered. If nothing had been done, the country would probably have become chaotic and it would have been impossible to rule. Among other manoeuvres, the government decided to modify its 'job reservation' policy with the obvious intention of opening enough spaces for black people to be co-opted into the economic system of South Africa. Specifically, the government hastily increased a black middle class. A large number of blacks have been brought into the mainstream of the South African economic capitalist system. This was done in a number of ways. The government simply abolished certain laws which prevented Blacks from working in certain white institutions. For example, before 1979, it would have been impossible for me to teach at a white university. Dr Mosala and Dr Mofokeng would not be teaching in a white university now if those laws had not been abolished.

As a result of these new job opportunities, many blacks are able to occupy certain positions hitherto disallowed and to increase their income. In similar ways, in industry, a number of people have been given opportunities to earn more money. In the teaching field, the government has tried to equalize the salary for those who have university degrees.

This was a very important move by the government, attempting to create a large cushion of a black middle class against the poverty stricken, revolutionary masses in South Africa. It is an important strategy in the effort to maintain the status quo.

The other important move by the government occurred in the early 1980s when it began to realize that it had to further divide the black community by co-opting the so-called 'coloureds' and Indians into the so-called Tricameral Parliament.[2] This was also an intentional attempt to divide the united black-'coloured'-Indian struggle that had been formed under the auspices of the Black Consciousness Movement in the 1970s. Though most blacks decided to oppose this governmental manoeuvre, nevertheless there were a number of blacks who were prepared to sell out their own community in order to become partners in this new parliamentary arrangement. So the 'black moderates' are being slowly co-opted and are becoming a problem for us in South Africa. This, to me, is an important attempt by the government to bring about the kind of change which they believe will be quite safe.

Not only has the government tried to bring the so-called 'coloureds' and Indians into Parliament, but the government is also seeking to co-opt the 'African moderates' in order to 'reform' apartheid. For example, you will find the moderates working through the homeland system or in the cities (the so-called urban councils and towns). The government has created new laws to transform the townships into 'cities'. In addition, the government decided to create a new law, enabling black people to own property in the cities through the so-called 99-year lease-hold system. And in 1985, they opened that up a little by permitting black urban dwellers the free-hold rights in addition to the 99-year lease hold. That means, the blacks in the 'cities' can now choose to own property through either of the two systems. All these legal maneuvres were intended to create a middle class and to separate the 'urban' blacks from the rural blacks. A number of blacks has been made to believe that in fact this is a new shift, a real change.

In addition, the government has devised another structure, the so-called 'Regional Services Councils', which will attempt to provide services to both white cities and black 'towns' on a much larger regional basis. Since black towns do not have the economic base on which to earn income through taxes, this new structure attempts to overcome this serious economic disadvantage by re-channelling some of the wealth blacks have produced in white cities back to the black townships, hoping thereby to upgrade social services there and hopefully to give credibility to the black 'town' councils. And here we find blacks, appointed by the government, becoming partners in the oppression of blacks in South Africa, thus preventing the birth of real democracy. We also have other formulas for example, during 1985-1986 in Natal, the government gave provisional approval for some blacks and whites to run their own state on a non-racial regional basis. Whether this will work out, we do not know because it is opposed by many whites who support the ruling National Party which for so long has been wedded to the ideology of ethnic politics of divide and rule.

In these ways the relaxations of certain governmental institutions try to bring in some blacks who, themselves, become instruments of oppression. As a result, there are debates today about the 'New Constitution' in South Africa and the 'protection of minority rights'. The government and its supporters are very much aware that they cannot run the country much longer. They are seeking a formula whereby they can hand over some power to a safe black government, provided their white minority rights are protected. By this they mean their economic, cultural and social privileges would be enshrined in the constitution. They hope to pursue a resolution similar to Zimbabwe's constitution. But we know these white privileges as in Zimbabwean experiment will eventually fall away.

To sum up: the government has encouraged the black middle class to work with it in order to devise cosmetic reforms. Such reforms are cosmetic precisely because they simply call for a modernization of apartheid. In each instance, whites would continue to dominate the majority if these new measures were to succeed. With these efforts, they hope to forestall the necessary changes that have to take place in South Africa.

Private Economic Reforms

On another level, we have other movements coming from the private enterprise economy. This economy has also been a partner working hand in glove with the government to create a middle class (e.g., the upgrading of black management who are paid good salaries). Again, the new black middle class has opted out of the struggle because the more they earn they, of course, acquire more property and personally they have more to lose. It is interesting to see how many of these black middle class people have become so conservative as to be almost immovable. They are becoming a serious problem, not only for the young people in South Africa but to all who are committed to fundamental change.

In addition, the private economy is pouring a great deal of money into organizations such as the Urban Foundation, whose mission is to ameliorate the black situation in the cities: to help create middle class housing and to relax the Group Areas Act (i.e., the legal separation of blacks and whites). Of course, this will only affect a very few people who can afford homes in the cities or in white suburbs. But the overwhelming majority of blacks will be left out. Furthermore, the private enterprise sector has been working very hard to open 'central business districts' in the white cities to black intrepreneurs with limited success. In the past, the government forbade blacks to run businesses in the cities. Now, through the creation of a middle class, the white capitalists try to encourage blacks to become partners in the racial capitalist system of South Africa.

Similarly, the government has created the 'small business development corporation' which gives loans to small businesses in order to also promote black capitalism. Because, as professor Cornel West's paper indicates, they realize that most South African movements are anti-capitalist. The government tries everything under the sun to subvert all progressive movements by its intensive focus on the establishment of a sizeable black middle class.

Furthermore, we do have two of our own black economic institutions. First, there is the National African Chamber of Commerce (NAFCOC) which also promotes black middle class capitalism. Second, there exists a black African bank which gives loans to blacks so that blacks can have a stake in the running of the South African economy. All of these private economic reforms project change, but change which would not benefit the masses of South Africa.

Attempts at Dialogue

There have been debates and attempts to promote dialogue in South Africa. We see movements to promote dialogue between white establishments and the African National Congress (ANC), which is perceived as the main opposition party in South Africa. For example, the white parliamentary oppositional group, the Progressive Federal Party (PFP), went to Lusaka in Zambia to meet ANC representatives. In the same way, we have South African business men (women have not been mentioned) going to Lusaka to consult with the ANC. Obviously they all realize that, at some stage in the future, they may have to reckon with the possibility of an ANC government. Consequently they hope to discover ways to have their bread buttered in such a future government. Thus you find some of the white English speaking liberals (e.g., the PFP) trying to protect white interests.

Moreover, some of the English liberal student movements and some Afrikaner student groups have also participated in these efforts to talk. Specifically in 1985, students at Stellenbosch University (an Afrikaner institution) attempted to organize a discussion. Even further, the Afrikaner leadership, like Dr De Lange, chairman of the Broederbond,[3] also met the ANC in New York in December 1985. Lately, Afrikaner academics and even sport administrators have defied the government by falling over each other as they vied to go to Lusaka to hold discussions with the ANC leadership. Thus forces in the white community seek to both neutralize the revolutionary nature of the ANC and bring out ANC 'moderates' (who supposedly are not Marxists) into dialogue. Of course, all of these schemes have now failed. The path toward 'evolutionary' change in South Africa will not mean a fundamental rearrangement.

Some of the white church leadership have expressed interests in dialogue along similar lines. Some church leaders have even encouraged dialogue between the government and the ANC. Of course, they argue that the ANC must *first* lay down its arms and then come to a conference table. However they do not call for the South African government to disarm itself.

Linked closely with dialogue, reconciliation has become a key phrase in South Africa. In fact, we have organizations like the National Initiative for Reconciliation (NIR) which, obviously, promotes the ideal of reconciliation in South Africa. Unfortunately, they do not seem to appreciate that without justice reconciliation will not be possible in a country where the dominant white section of the society has benefitted for centuries at the expense of the black majority. In any case, even some white liberals have resigned from Parliament and formed a new organization called the Institute of Democratic Alternatives. All these projects try to find compromises or formulas whereby some form of change can take place which would accommodate white economic interests.

Also, there are other groups who organize themselves on a very small level, at a tea. They drink tea together and find one another there. I do not know what they will eventually do. In the past, this was tried and, of course, failed. The Black Consciousness Movement said no to this. Certainly we blacks have tea and cakes in our own homes. Why should we go and drink tea in white houses, hoping thereby to realize change in apartheid?

The People's Resistance

Over against these 'dialogues', capitalist economic reforms, and governmental maneuvering stands the people's movement committed to radical changes in South Africa. The most important of these (as correctly argued by Professor West's paper) would be the student revolt which has been going on since 1984. Most students sacrifice their very fruitful years to fight for liberation. Black student groups commit themselves to total rejection of apartheid, the whole economic system and social institutions. In fact, they have coined the slogan 'liberation now and education later' because they feel all the structures do not benefit black people. Basically, they desire fundamental change and a redistribution of power. They realize that in South Africa today, even if Chief Gatsha Buthelezi,[4] became the next president, very little would change. Because what is really at stake in South Africa is the economy. Unfortunately some blacks feel that if we simply bring about a change of the white Afrikaner government and leave the economic system intact, then everything will be fine. We will then have utopia. But this will not come about in South Africa.

On the contrary, many people realize that the real struggle is round the economy; whoever controls the money in South Africa controls the future.

Consequently, many people are committed to working for change at the economic level as well. So we have labour unions which have become a very important force for change in South Africa and have become a battleground for blacks. Along with labour, we have developed the consumer boycotts, hitting the economy so hard that most investors lost capital in 1985.

In fact, attacks on the apartheid economy have had a very serious impact. Specifically, it has brought about a serious recession. A number of companies in the United States and in Europe, who had previously opposed disinvestment, have now disinvested. For instance in 1985, 39 American companies divested. In 1986, General Motors, IBM, the British Barclay's Bank, and a Canadian shoe company, all, among others, disinvested. Of course they did not take such actions because of moral reasons. They only use a moral rationale as a smokescreen to cover their economic losses. On the contrary, the people's resistance *inside* South Africa organized itself at the labour front, and through economic boycotts made it impossible for these monopoly corporations to reap profits any more. In brief, the South African people forced them to leave our country.

We also have other movements such as the United Democratic Front (UDF) and the Azanian Peoples Organization (AZAPO). It will be the convergence, it seems to me, of a number of movements — the student sector, the labour organizations, the consumer boycott groups, political activities of the UDF and AZAPO, and the liberation movement, — all together pressuring the South African government to the extent that they will break the camel's back.

Precisely because of this convergence, the Afrikaners are desperate. Obviously the government's declaration of the state of emergency admits they can no longer run the country. But I do not think they will fall in the foreseeable future. Yet we should note the significant points made by the liberation movement (e.g., the ability to infiltrate in spite of the difficulties and hit at certain key places). Moreover, the very fact that almost every week the army and the police discover different types of arms and caches indicates the growth of the guerrilla movement in South Africa.

Because of all this, it did not surprise me when, during 1986, the British government pushed for a 'Zimbabwean' solution whereby Nelson Mandela would be released and there would have been dialogue between the apartheid government and the liberation movement. I think for the West's own economic concerns, it has become necessary for both Britain and the United States to produce a formula to protect their economic interests. Whether they will succeed, I am not sure.

To conclude like Prof West, I wish to refer to a group of church people in South Africa who work very, very hard to bring about change. They are among others the Kairos theologians[5] who have been on the cutting edge of change. By pressing for a fundamental realignment in society, they have denied the South African government the legitimacy it has always enjoyed. Because they believe South African institutions are so evil and cannot be reformed, they specifically argue for and encourage a just revolution. Evil needs to be removed. Therefore the people's resistance movement will some day bring about a fundamentally new order. It must certainly come!

FOOTNOTES

1. See Alan Brooks and Jeremy Brickhill *Whirlwind Before the Storm, the origins and development of the uprising in Soweto and the rest of South Africa from June to December 1976 (London: International Defence and Aid Fund for Southern Africa, 1980);* and Baruch Hirson *Year of Fire and Year of Ash, the Soweto revolt: roots of a revolution?* (London: Zed Press, 1979).
2. A national parliament created by the apartheid government in 1984. Supposedly a reform measure, the parliament allows for white, 'coloured' and Indian members. Not only does the white minority control the parliament, the country's black majority is totally excluded.
3. The Afrikaner secret society which controls all Afrikaner interest in the religious, political, governmental, cultural, economic, social, and civic sectors of South Africa. The Broederbond, literally meaning brotherhood, is the chief architect behind apartheid.
4. The Chief heads KwaZulu bantustan or 'homeland'. The South African government attempts to utilize the Chief and his Inkatha organization to stop progressive moves toward meaningful change in South Africa.
5. A group of theologians who produced the famous *Kairos Document* in September 1985.

7

Theological Reflection on Black Theology

James H. Cone

During my visit to South Africa in the summer of 1985, I received a brief but very lasting impression of what it means to be black in a society where black people have no rights which white people are bound to respect. Now, of course, my first experiences of white racism began during my childhood in the southern part of the United States. But my experience in South Africa completely changed my feeling about my own place and made me realize that the experience in the south was nothing like South Africa. It is an experience that I will never forget and which I have written something about.

And it is not my intention to give a formal paper on the origin of black liberation theology. Rather, I want to have an opportunity to engage professor Mofokeng and the paper he has given to us. Moreover, I and persons like Gayraud Wilmore have written about the history and the origin of black theology in many books and articles. I merely want to say that contemporary black theology began in the socio-political context of black people's struggle for justice in the United States in the 1960s. It did not come into being from seminary professors or university scholars when they decided to write books about it. On the contrary, it began in the context of a fight, a struggle for survival and liberation in a land (somewhat like South Africa) in which black people were treated less than fully human. North American black theology, therefore, came out of black people's movement for liberation as we attempted to make sense out of it and to deal with the problem of identity which that movement certainly enhanced.

Black Theology: Martin and Malcolm

No one described the black American problem any sharper than the lives of two persons: Martin King and Malcolm X. Indeed, the problem can be summarized in two very famous statements which they have given. Martin King stated:

> *I have a dream that one day this nation will rise up and live out the true meaning of its creed, 'We hold these truths to be self-evident, that all [people] are created equal.'.... With this faith we will be able to work together, pray together, to struggle together, to go to jail together, to stand up for freedom together, knowing that we will be free one day.... This will be the day when all God's children will be able to sing with a new meaning, 'my country 'tis of thee, sweet land of liberty, of thee I sing.'*

But there is another voice in the 1960s that saw it differently. In contrast to King, Malcolm X believed:

> *No, I'm not an American. I'm one of the 22 million black people who are victims of Americanism, one of the victims of democracy, nothing but disguised hypocrisy. So, I'm not standing here speaking to you as an American, or a patriot, or a flag-saluter, or a flag-waver — no, not I! I'm speaking as a victim of this American system. And I see America through the eyes of the victim. I don't see an American dream. I see an American nightmare!*

These two persons represent the two sharply contrasting views of America that distinctly defined the 1960s. Martin King, the unquestioned king of the Civil Rights Movement, was an integrationist and a Christian minister who, during most of his ministry, saw America as essentially a dream as yet fulfilled. King dreamed of a land where people of different races and all nationalities and creeds would live together as brothers and sisters. On the other hand, Malcolm X, the unquestioned spokesperson for the disinherited black masses of the northern ghettoes, was a separatist and a Muslim minister who viewed America as a realized nightmare in which black people experienced political oppression, economic exploitation, and social degradation at the hands of white people. Martin King saw America in terms of what this nation could become if black people and white people of goodwill assumed their political responsibility in implementing the freedom inherent in what he saw in the Declaration of Independence and the Constitution. But Malcolm X saw America in terms of this nation's past and current treatment of its people of color; 244 years as slaves followed by a colonized status that offered blacks no economic security, political power, or social respect in a society defined by white supremacy.

Thus in the writings and lives of Martin and Malcolm, we see two Americas. One view of America is based on faith in the American political system and the Christian hope that blacks and whites could work together in the creation of, what Martin King called, the 'Beloved Community'. And the other was based on the past cruelties of American slavery and the present reality of the urban ghetto, a clear indication that white people had no intention of recognizing the basic humanity of black people. Martin's unrealized dream and Malcolm's persistent nightmare, these two ideas of America collided in the 1960s. From this collision emerged black theology. Black theology, then, is an attempt to reconcile these two apparent contradictions in the black community: Martin King and Malcolm X, integration and separation. Malcolm represents the 'black' in black theology. And Martin King represents the 'theology' in that phrase.

The tensions found in Martin and Malcolm and in black theology are deeply rooted in black history in this country. No one described the tension any sharper than WEB Du Bois' famous and classical statement in 1903 when he said:

> It is a peculiar sensation, this double-consciousness, this sense of always looking at one's self through the eyes of others, of measuring one's soul by the tape of a world that looks on in amused contempt and pity. One ever feels [this] twoness, – an American, a

Negro; two souls, two thoughts, two unreconciled strivings; two warring ideals in one dark body, whose dogged strength alone keeps it from being torn asunder.

It is precisely these two warring ideas that produced black theology. We were attempting to make peace with them. As we know now and as I try to say in my classes at Union Seminary, all theology begins when people decide to reflect upon the ultimate meaning of their attempt to make sense out of their lives. Living in a society that did not recognize our dignity and our wealth as blacks, black people decided to rise up in protest and to claim our right to be black. 'I'm black and I'm proud' became a slogan of the young and the old, the men and the women, the Christian and the non-Christian. Because blackness was the most visible symbol of our oppression, it became the most important symbol in defining our understanding of the theological task.

Furthermore, when oppressed people begin to do theology, they must begin not with some universal principle discovered in research by some professor, but rather their theological reflection (e.g., theological reflection among the victims) must begin at the point where they are struggling to eliminate their hurts and their pains. That is why we called it black theology. So black theology began primarily with its focus on race. And now, of course, we realize that that focus alone is too limited. We need to enlarge it. We have begun to try to do that with the focus on class analysis and the problem of sexism, including homophobia and also global problems within the context of the Ecumenical Association of Third World Theologians (EATWOT) and other international contexts.

However, the focus on these other issues do not minimize the importance of race. In fact, such a focus enhances an appreciation for the racial concern and makes it more important. Again, no one illustrates this better than the lives of Martin King and Malcolm X. For they tell us what it means to be open to the truth and also to die for it. The experiences of other people which they share with us is a gift, a gift from God through them. To deny this gift is to reject the other person and to reject the other person is to reject

God, the one who is indeed the mother, the nurturer, the sustainer, the creator of us all. God meets us in the other person and embraces us there. There is no other way to know God existentially except by meeting God in others, in their struggles, in their histories as they seek to be who they were created to be.

Common Concerns for Black Theology

I first encountered black theology in South Africa primarily through others; archbishop Tutu, Allan Boesak, and others who came through New York City in the early part of the 1970s. Consequently I was empowered by their struggle to make sense out of their context as I was attempting to do so in mine. Of course there is diversity between the theologies in South Africa and the United States because our experiences are different. And neither of us has the whole truth. We are still searching for our way to that truth. Therefore we cannot be expected to agree on every political and theological point. But the fact that we are here in this three day conference means that our commonality is much more significant than our differences. We are engaged in a common struggle for justice that is empowered by our common faith in the God who is the creator of us all.

I want to end by posing certain questions to us as we continue our work here and as we leave to continue our work in our respective places. I want to underline some questions or some issues that have emerged in the contexts of both theologies to which I think we need to give much more serious reflection. The first one I want to mention is sexuality. Black theology and the black church in both the USA and in South Africa cannot avoid this issue in their struggle for holistic liberation. Obviously Kelly Brown and Roxanne Jordan from USA and South Africa respectively made this point crystal clear in their papers, and other black women in both contexts do so as well. It is not easy for us as men to face it honestly, seriously and with the integrity that it needs. But wholeness in sexuality involves more than just the relation between men and women. In addition, it involves the relation between women and women and men and men, as gays and lesbians are teaching us. We cannot avoid these issues. The question we want to ask is: are we, as black theologians in the US and in South Africa going to be reactionary and join similar forces in the Catholic church and among white conservative evangelicals? I hope not. I hope we create some space and some time for more creative reflection.

The second issue is the question of race and class. Now no issue has been more hotly debated in the black community than this one. It has been the source of many divisions in the black history in the US and is currently having a disabling effect in South Africa. How can it be resolved in a way that we can disagree without being disagreeable, as Martin King would ask? Both Martin and Malcolm were kept separated (they met only once for a few minutes) largely on the basis of issues closely related to the ones involved in the conflicts between race and class. I am convinced that the black political struggle was disenabled in the early 1970s partly because of the theoretical splits on race and class analysis. And a similar tragedy, as we have heard in this conference and other times, is happening within the context of South Africa among nationalists and multi-racialist persons.

The third issue that I think we need to face is the one that focuses on Scripture. No document has caused more problems than Scripture. It is ambiguous in its message. And this ambiguity is deeply embedded in black history. Part of the bible can be sources of empowerment for the oppressed and other parts can contribute to their oppression. For instance, Howard Thurman, one of the great black theologians and preachers of our time, tells the story of his grandmother who asked him not to read certain parts of the Scripture to her, especially apostle Paul. And when he asked her about that, she told him it was because of Paul's claim that women and slaves ought to be obedient to their masters and she did not want to hear these Pauline passages because she had heard similar reading during the time of slavery. Therefore she commanded him not to read Paul to her. But I have also learned from South Africans, from feminists, from gay and lesbian theologians; they have shown how deeply this ambiguity is embedded in the message of Scripture itself. Now the question we have to ask is: what is the authority of this document, this scripture, in the development of a liberation theology in the black community? I do not know. I want to hear more dialogue about that. In fact, it has been raised and engaged throughout this conference.

Fourth, what can we learn from the experience of others, especially in the third world in the doing of theology today? EATWOT has reinforced for me the importance of the global context for doing theology. For me, it has emphasized the necessity to engage the global dimension of theology by relating black theology to other minorities, other than blacks, within the context of the United States itself.

The fifth and last issue is: how do we get black theology from the seminaries to the churches? What is wrong with black church leadership in both countries and with black theologians in both contexts that prevent the teaching of black theology in so many churches? How can we begin to bridge the gap between what we can say in the seminary and what is preached on Sunday morning? These are several important questions which I believe need further discussion between black theology in the USA and in South Africa.

8

Black Theological Perspectives, Past And Present.

Takatso A. Mofokeng

Introduction

The people of South Africa are living in difficult times when crucial decisions have to be made. With the state of emergency broadened to include the entire Black South Africa (there are no signs of it in white towns) there is no doubt that there is a great measure of intransigence and desperation on the part of the white state. Large-scale indiscriminate detentions of Black leaders and activists of all ages; tear-gassing of people in churches and at funeral services; the brutal shootings of unarmed school children; these all provide irrefutable concrete evidence of this intransigence and desperation. Black South Africa has been forced to go back to a low level of resistance because of increasing and deepening repression and harassment. This situation of crisis has brought Black politicians, economists, social scientists, religious leaders and theologians who are in prison as well as those who are still outside, to a tactical stop. They have had to stop and review this situation of apparent stalemate and search for new and more meaningful answers to pertinent questions which are posed by it and devise new strategies of advancing the cause of liberation.

The present setback which we are experiencing in our Exodus is also an opportunity which cannot be lost. It is a setback in that what appeared, a year ago, to be an unstoppable thrust to bring about the emergence of a new future and the birth of a new nation has been abruptly and ruthlessly blocked. While it is a lamentable setback, it is one which can, and has to, be converted into an opportunity which, if properly and carefully utilized, could benefit the struggle for liberation. The state of emergency is for Black people, an epistemological moment to which all thought and language have come. It is not certain anymore that old theological language and communal activity will continue to be the best ways of expressing the presence of God among the oppressed in the most effective manner in and beyond the present state of emergency. It is no longer certain that this language which used to kindle the light of hope and the fire of active faith in the oppressed, will continue to be the most effective witness to God as God continues to bring down opposition to God's sovereignty and to the liberation of God's oppressed creation. It is also no longer certain that this theological language which we now use will continue through the entire state of emergency to give appropriate expression to, and even inspire, new 'emergency' responses of Black people to God's command to engage in a radical discipleship in pursuance of justice and liberation.

It is therefore imperative that, in our attempt to be theologically vigilant and our continuing obligation to test and reconcile black concrete discipleship with verbal articulation of that discipleship, we should grab the epistemological moment which has been forced upon the Black theological community and struggle. While standing firmly in the present, we have to re-examine the past in order to fashion a better and crisper and sharper theological language that can cut open the door to a future of liberation for the Black people of South Africa.

Light On Methodology In Black Theology

From 1978 when, according to Steve Biko, 'essentially the black community is a very religious community, which often reflects on beings, in other words, what is my purpose in life, why am I here, who am I'?;[1] going through 1980 when Bonganjalo Goba stated that ' ... black theological reflection as a communal praxis cannot be separated from the ongoing commitment to political change in South Africa';[2] to 1986 when Itumeleng Mosala asserted that Black Theology has to be a theoretical weapon of struggle in the hands of the exploited Black masses;[3] this theology has always been a theology of praxis which emerged in the heat of the historical struggles of black Christian workers and peasants and has always retained that base. Initially, however, the link with this praxis was not pronounced and vivid because black praxis had not yet evolved into a deliberately organized historical project. But as soon as the South African Student Organization (SASO) and the Black People's Convention (BPC) launched the earliest concrete social projects for purposes of economic upliftment and psychological liberation under the banner of Black Consciousness, this important methodological link became explicit and visible. It immediately had a direct and forceful impact on the determination and arrangement of theological themes in order of priority. In fact Black Theology, as a theological articulation of Black consciousness in the religious realm became one of the many projects of conscientization. It continues to play an important role in the ideological formation of the black political agents. This is evidenced by the successful leadership of archbishop Desmond Tutu, Dr. Alan Boesak and other Black clergy.

This complex relationship was misunderstood by white theologians who wrongly attempted to link Black Theology with some European theologies in order to acquire the right of placing it on their agenda in the arena of their struggle for orthodoxy[4]

As a matter of fact the blame cannot be put entirely on the acquisitive instinct of European and other western theologians. Black theologians in South Africa are also to blame. They did not make the distinction between their theology and others sufficiently clear. They also continued to use dominant theological categories which are household categories in European theology without even explaining the difference that emerges when the same categories are used in their theology. Neither did they make a total break epistemologically with European theology. They continued to be dependent on it for a long time and thereby opened their theology for European theological meddling, long before they were ready to deal with critique from outside.

James Cone, a Black American theologian, was very clear from the very beginning that he was not satisfied with Euro-American theology and that he was attempting to leave it behind him. His *A*

Black Theology of Liberation is evidence of this noble effort. In that way other black theologians who shared the same concern could come in and say whether he had succeeded in his goal or not. This is how G.Wilmore and C. Cone came into this debate and assisted J.Cone through their critique to go further and complete the epistemological break which he had initiated and make a real new beginning for Black Theology.[5]

It was the case on the issue of the identity of Black Theology. Wilmore asked for factors that made Black theology Black and thus distinguished it from white theology. He pushed Cone to get to the basic issue of the sources and the norm, which is what determines the identity, content and methodology of a theology.

In the above mentioned book J Cone can be seen vigorously grappling with the theological constructions of K Barth, P Tillich and, to a lesser extent, that of R Niebhur. He criticizes some parts of their theology in the light of the social challenges and theological needs of the Black community and appropriates some of its useful methodological elements. In that way Cone released himself from the grip of Euro-American theology and went further in his development of Black Theology, as it is evident especially in his book, *God of the Oppressed*. South African Black theologians were not so fortunate in that regard. They did not have a Wilmore at that very early and crucial stage of the development of their Black theology. Consequently their theology suffered from a lack of self-criticism which did not last very long as we can see from the present debates among black theologians in South Africa.

When most Black theologians focused, as a matter of priority, their entire attention on the Black community and its praxis as sources of material for reflection, and neglected public methodological debates, B Goba plunged into these debates in which he was later joined by I Mosala and B Tlhagale who lifted the debate to a higher level. At a time when the acting subject in the struggle for liberation was not yet clearly identifiable in group or class terms B Goba, M Buthelezi, D Tutu and others consistently identified the entire Black community as the acting subject of its liberation.[6] It was only later when Black trade unions for both men and women made a forceful appearance on the labour scene and took their rightful place at the forefront of the fierce battle for a society of unshackled people that Mosala and Tlhagale identified our interlocutor as the black workers.[7] It is necessary to say that this change of the identity of the acting subject did not imply disillusionment, with or a rejection of, the black community. It was a necessary deepening of the concept 'Black community' whereby this community is named in relation to the primary activity - economic activity - that determines its oppression and also serves as a trustworthy criterion of national liberation. Black people have been dispossessed of their land which is the basic means of all production and subsistence as well as a source of power. They have been turned into dispossessed workers whose only possession is their labour power. By identifying black people as workers these theologians have lifted our struggle beyond civil rights to human rights, from an exclusive struggle against racism to a social and national revolution.

This deepening by the identifying of the black interlocutor as the Black worker is very important for black theology. It introduces theology into the area of the material basis of theology which has been somewhat neglected by Euro-American theologians in favour of spiritualization. This is, to my mind, an important theological deepening and corrective.

Recent publications by our American brothers and sisters also show evidence of a further development in this area.[8] In the earlier stages of the development of their version of black theology the interlocutor was the black community as a whole. The acute and urgent problem was racism as it affected the entire black community and as it permeates the entire fabric of American society. This viewpoint was carried forward into international theological dialogues, especially into the dialogue with Latin American theologians where it was presented forcefully by Cone and Wilmore among others. Latin Americans on their part approached theology from the class paradigm and also forcefully presented class as the determinant in society.[9]

In the ensuing difficult debate it took time before positions softened, both sides accepted the point made by the other side. Black theologians recognized that racism is not the sole problem facing blacks but also that capitalism posed a serious problem and that it had to be addressed theologically, combated socially as well as politically, and eradicated simultaneously with racism. What is important for us at this stage of our discussion is that, in addition to convincingly presenting the painful concrete issue of racism and acknowledging that the Latin Americans had a point about capitalism, Black Americans also addressed the issues of the religion of the oppressed as well as the culture of the oppressed within the framework of Marxism. They pointed out that these two areas are the achilles' heel of Marxism.[10] In fact as far as religion is concerned Marxism generally regards it a negative factor in the life of oppressed people, that is, as an ideological instrument that is used by the dominant classes against the dominated classes. As we all can attest from our own experience as well as that of many people in our black communities, this is not completely true. Oppressed Black people continuously remold religious ideas which are imposed upon them and produce a religion that is capable of functioning as a defensive as well as a combative ideological weapon. [11]

This position is based, as we know, on the Marxian principle that dominant ideas in every society are the ideas of the dominant class. This leads to ignoring ideas of the oppressed or relegating them to a position of insignificance in the entire society including the dominated classes thus clearing the field for the dominant ideas to dominate unchallenged. The experience of the oppressed is that their ideas, in the present case their dominated religion, continues to survive and play a sustaining role as well as that of contesting the hegemony of the religion of the dominant classes. (So far the Italian communist party is the only Marxist party that has acknowledged the positive role of religion, especially the religion of the oppressed.)

The implication of the above for Black social analysts is that Black theologians and other social analysts should not rely exclusively on Marxism in their attempt to understand their predicament in a capitalist and racist world.They have to find within their own cultural heritage other tools which will be used complementarily with Marxism.

This is a lesson which is very important for South African Black theologians to learn because there is a significant section of the oppressed in South Africa today which insists on the validity of the orthodox Marxian assertion that race is not a co-determinant of oppression of Black people. Those who hold that view are bound to ignore the culture and religion of Black people in their search for weapons of struggle.

The redefinition of the identity of the Black community also coincided with a new issue on the agenda - women's oppression and their struggle against it. Black Theology had up to that point not addressed it and for this gross neglect Black theologians have to hang their heads in shame and ask for God's forgiveness and that of our mothers and sisters. All attention had up to that point focused entirely on national issues in which Black people as a group stand over and against white people, white economy and the white state. Even Black women at a time when they too were in the forefront of the battle facing the wrath of the army and the police and suffering equally if not more, demanded the issue of their subservient position during times of relative peace to be addressed. The entire Black community, especially men, were challenged to widen and deepen sanctificatory processes within itself and practice internal justice and distribute power to effect equality in order to enhance the external thrust of communal praxis and theology in the combat against oppressive forms of white theology. Black women who have tasted equality in battle, in suffering and in victory are not prepared to return to their former status in the community and at home after combat or when the struggle is over. They called for internal dialogue to redress this situation so that the gains of their struggle would not be lost.[12]

The church and theology have not escaped from this justifiable criticism. It is indeed true that Black women constitute the largest group in the church and also that they provide the material means for the survival of the church. But, paradoxically, they are the objects of a male created, monitored and imposed power structure and theology. Women are, in most cases, not allowed to exercise power in the church in which they are almost the sole audience and activists, be it political, religious, financial or theological power.

Women are allocated some space yes, but it is space at some remote corner and not at the centre stage of the church. That remote corner is the only space they are allowed to use for articulation of their own theology, a theology which they create in response to the challenges which face them specifically as well as those which face their families and community. Black women in South African churches are starting to stand up against this exclusion in church and theology. They have started to articulate their theological thoughts and demand an audience and dialogue.

As we are all aware, and have come to accept, doing a relevant theology demands a rigorous analysis of society. This is the area in which the overwhelming majority of Black women in South African churches are, in my opinion, not yet well grounded. And this is the area in which Black American women are well advanced. They can, therefore, be of great assistance to Black South African church women and theologians.

As we have already stated, the advance to which we are referring is in the area of the analysis of society and this determines the questions and priorities for the theological agenda. We have noticed that Black female theologians in the US distinguish their predicament from that of white women. This is because of the peculiar way in which racism operates in a capitalist society. It leads to more suffering for Black women in society. On the other side, capitalism in a racist society favours white women and exploits black women together with Black men as well as the entire Black community.

This understanding of their society has led to a development of Black theology from a feminist perspective which is different and separate from white feminist theology[13] Its agenda is also different from that of white feminist theology because Black women stand in the black community and the Black church. They are not indistinguishable members of American society and church. This is what most black South African women of the church still have to learn, accept and defend. Since feminist theology came to South Africa wearing a white garb and was introduced by white feminist theologians at a time when the Black consciousness perspective had lost ground to the so called progressive democratic perspective, women's theological reflection is also being dominated by the dominant perspective and the questions and priorities of white society and the white church. Black questions take a back seat as a result.

The social developments in South Africa have inevitably led to a greater appreciation of the value of the social sciences and their analytical usefulness in bringing clarity to an often muddy and confusing situation. Goba in the past called, and at presently Tlhagale and Mosala call repeatedly for a search for an appropriate biblical hermeneutic which would deal with these new issues satisfactorily. It is especially Mosala's timely criticism of Black Theology on its failure to become the property of the masses that really hurt. Black Theology, he said fairly recently, quoting K Marx,' ... has not yet become a material force because it has not gripped the masses'.[14] He called for a new way of going about the biblical text, a way that will enable the hidden and silenced but struggling oppressed people in biblical communities to become visible, and to break their silence and speak up clearly and loudly enough to be heard by the equally silenced black people today as they stand up to demand God's justice and liberation. As history shows, radical calls of this nature are not readily heard or speedily responded to. Black theologians in South Africa are, however, slowly responding and in their struggle to read Scripture in the light of the perspective of the black working people as their loyal 'organic intellectuals' they are amazed at the dynamite that lies hidden deep in the bowels of the scriptural text. It will, however, take some time before the results of this new effort reach the international theological market in large quantities.

Inevitably, the above hermeneutical question raises again a related issue which, we thought, had been adequately dealt with and closed in the 1970s by A Boesak, T Mofokeng and others, namely the relationship between scripture and a social praxis which is informed by social sciences, especially by the dialectical sociology of Marxian derivation.[15] While Boesak, in his argument with Cone in the 1970s, insisted that 'the light of the Word of God' is the only final judgement of all action and reflection, other Black theologians disagreed and contended that light shines both ways because of the unifying and enlightening presence of Jesus the Messiah in the struggles of faith of both the communities in the biblical text as well as that of the suffering Black people of South Africa whose text is being written with their blood.

It's interesting to see that Black theologians in the United States have also had a similar debate. I am thinking here of J Cone and Deotis Roberts.[16] In this debate Cone took the position that God is not absent from the life of the oppressed as they struggle in life and as they read the scriptures in the light of their actual concrete actions, and that consequently, that practice is of revelational importance. In other words the light of that practice shines on the scriptural text making certain things in the text perceptible as the light of the latter does on the practice, improving it qualitatively and driving it forward. Roberts, I think, takes the traditional reformed view that light can only shine from the Bible, which is the view propounded by Boesak in his first book *Farewell to Innocence*.

I am of the opinion that, when discussing this matter we should bring the Spirit of God into the picture and ask what the role of the Spirit is in communal practice as the Spirit who dwells among those who are occupied with being obedient to Jesus' command of loving their neighbour. If this Spirit is God and if this God is, as the Bible teaches, involved in that communal practice in both its concrete and theoretical forms, is it too far-fetched to conclude that the Spirit of God brings the two practices together? To put it differently, I do not see how and why the spirit of God can be involved in the life and practice of the biblical community of faith as well as in the contemporary community of faith and not be involved in bringing the two communities together when the contemporary community desires to hold dialogue with, and learn, from its predecessors. I think that the God who has promised us his presence continues to use our own practice to enlighten our reading of the scriptural text. I would therefore agree with Cone on this matter.

For those who fear contemporary textual domination of the biblical text and want to protect it, I would say that we should emphasize the dynamic character and nature of the Spirit of God in the community of faith. God's Spirit cannot be held hostage or prisoner in the practice or life of the contemporary community just as this same Spirit could not be imprisoned in the biblical communities. The bible witnesses to many occasions and situations where people or communities were abandoned by God and whom the Spirit of God deserted. The spirit of God is both free and frees.

Coupled with the above issue is the closely related one of the 'authority' of scripture as a whole which Mosala, especially, addresses very provocatively and poses very pertinent questions. According to him, too many Black theologians still approach the text with awe as the 'Word of God' and consequently use, uncritically, texts which can have no other impact than that of frustrating the total liberation of Black people.[17] This mystification of the text still stands in the way of it being read rationally, and appropriated with a liberating effect. It hides the class struggles which were going on in biblical communities of which the text reports. It also hides the fact that the text itself is a product of such struggles, one that has to be approached with great analytical care, lest Black theologians make wrong textual connections. Unfortunately we can only report that not many of our theologians, especially biblical scholars, have entered this discussion. It is therefore not evident whether this proposed approach will make Black Theology grip the black Christian masses and enhance their faith as well as stimulate and radicalize their struggle for justice and liberation.

Black American theologians approach the scriptural text from within the black church and read it using all the available reading tools from within this church. This is important because it is this church or christians within it who read that text and have to be helped to understand it better and apply it to life. So far evidence has shown that this community has always read this text in such a way that it contributed to their struggle to survive in a society which militated against the life of black people and denied their humanity. Their reading has even encouraged them to engage as Wilmore has shown so clearly in his Black Religion and Black Radicalism, in different acts of rebellion in the past and present. There was therefore no general opiating influence of the bible evident.[18]

But since many black people belong to the working class and are aware of their class position and class interests have to be reached with the biblical text, it remains a question whether they can be reached and impressed with the traditional reading of this text. I have doubts. I would suspect that they would prefer to read it in such a way that they would hear it as addressing their working class problems which are not absolutely identical with those of the black community per se. If that be the case, then black American theologians will benefit from engaging in the dialogue which Mosala is calling for.

Deepening The Sources

Right from the inception of contemporary Black Theology the definition of the concept 'black' has been problematic. While there was unanimity right at the beginning that all the oppressed black people of South Africa, that is, Africans, the so-called Coloureds and Indians - are black people, the same cannot be said regarding inclusion of black culture, black history and African traditional religion in Black Theology as formative factors. M. Buthelezi explicitly and emphatically talked about the culture of blacks having been totally destroyed - and was followed by A Boesak in that he excluded it in his first book while including black history. Steve Biko on the other hand firmly held that black culture had only been severely damaged but not totally erased from the memory of the oppressed or removed from their daily lives.[19] Many theologians including those who contributed towards the publication: *A relevant theology for Africa* concurred with him on this.[20] At the end one was confronted by two parallel streams in our black theological thinking which still persist despite slight convergence lately. Many black theologians of the former persuasion have come to acknowledge the pervasiveness of black culture as well as recognize the importance of black history for Black Theology. Those who were first in regarding black culture as important were already sifting through it to distinguish useful elements from those which would, if displayed to whites, wrongly give an impression of our readiness to submit to white oppression. Others were searching for cultural parallels with the culture of the Hebrew people of the Old as well as New Testament and identifying concepts like 'corporate personality' and 'solidarity' which are central to African and Hebrew perception of being human. Simon Maimela even explored the contribution which an African concept of salvation can make towards Christianity in general and to theology in particular.[21]

The case of African traditional religions was more difficult especially as it is found in the African Independent Churches - the principal religious custodians of African culture and traditional religion. Some students in SASO during the early days of the Black Consciousness Movement were rightly very critical of the African Independent Churches for their apolitical stance which significantly reduced the numbers of Black Christians in the forefront of the struggle. They subsequently advocated the total eradication of these churches, a task which would have been impossible given their close relationship with the black working class and working class conditions that still exist. The situation has fortunately changed, though not significantly. Notwithstanding persistent criticism of these churches' intolerable neutrality which is tantamount to support of the racist state, there is an increasing understanding among a significant number of black theologians of these churches and appreciation of their positive role in enabling the lowest in the black community to at least absorb the sting of oppression and survive.[22] We therefore anticipate an increase in interest and research in this area of church activity as well as dialogue with theologians and religious leaders of these churches on the part of black theologians. One can only caution that this new appreciation should not lead to an idealization of these churches. They still have great problems like all the historic churches.

As we all know, the areas of African culture, history and traditional religions have been areas of unhappy separation as well as possible bases of Pan African dialogue, co-operation and unification of black people in the world. In the 1970s there was, unfortunately, less success in the dialogue which went on between Afro-Americans and many Africans who took part in it. While G Wilmore and James Cone tried hard to bridge the differences by pointing at areas of possible common interest and cross fertilization, John Mbiti on the African side seemed irrevocably bent on widening the gap by stressing the differences between these theologies at the expense of commonalities.[23] It was not until Bishop Desmond Tutu entered this discussion as an African and a black person, that is, as one who combines in his life and thought African culture and politico-economic commitment on the African continent, that prospects for Pan-Africanism in theology improved. Since that intervention by a black South African, many of his countrymen have joined the discussion and more African theologians in free Africa accept the validity of the criticism made by James Cone that African theology is impoverished by neglect of socio-political issues. We are thinking here of people like J Chipenda, Kwesi Dickson and Jean Marc Ela. This shows the key strategic position which our situation of oppression and our struggle have put South African black theologians in this Pan-African theological dialogue. It remains to be seen whether we will live up to the challenges that face us and use opportunities which are open to us.

In their own appropriation of African culture, history and traditional religion as formative factors, some black theologians in South Africa are going further and consistently apply class analysis on them in order to eliminate their negative elements and discover positive ones. This they do notwithstanding recognition of the weakness of Marxism on issues of culture and religion. Mosala asserts for instance, regarding culture and black theology, that 'for this reason the task of a black theology of liberation is, amongst other things, to identify the distinctive forms of working class culture and use them as a basis for developing theological strategies of liberation'. When doing this we should search in the past struggles of our working people how this culture informed and transformed their struggles so that we can deal critically with their contemporary culture. It is necessary to do that because, as Marx says, "the history of all hitherto existing society is the history of class struggles". We should therefore investigate the cultural history of the struggling classes and learn from it. This is how Cornel West and James Cone deal with black culture in the United States [23].

As far as African history is concerned, I am of the opinion that, while we accept the symbolic importance of certain African personalities of the past as bearers of the tradition of struggle against oppression in its many different manifestations, we should dig deeper and unearth the real bearers of those struggles, the lowliest men, women and children in our African societies of the past and be informed by them in our reading of scripture and subsequent formulation of black theology. We should not get stuck in valorization of African feudal kings especially in present day South Africa where most of their descendents are being co-opted into the apartheid system and are consequently a serious distortion of the history of their forebears..

As far as African traditional religion is concerned, as it is practised inside as well as outside of the African Independent Churches we should be very careful especially now. Too many missionaries and former missionaries who were actually denying the validity of these religions and actively campaigned against them are now glorifying them. In the past they tried hard to elicit black support in their campaign to eradicate these religions, now they are again asking for black support for the rehabilitation of these religions. This we should not do. Instead we should follow our own path and critically appropriate only those elements which appeal to and sustain the black poor and most powerless in their struggle for survival. These we should consider incorporating into black theology.

Dominant Themes Of The Past And Present

Racist oppression and capitalist dispossession of blacks in South Africa has always undergone a historical development and manifested itself differently during different historical periods. This has happened, of course, in such a way that the suffering of our people broadened and worsened progressively. Not only men and women became the victims but old people and babies as well. The different official names which were used to refer to the indigenous people reflect this. They were initially called kaffirs, then natives, later bantu and now Blacks (with a truncated connotation). In their resistance black leaders kept a vigilant eye on the worsening situation. They worked hard to create an appropriate psychological resistance among blacks and also made necessary adjustments in their methods of resistance, continually evolved new strategies in order to be more effective in such worsening conditions. Since assault on blacks was not limited to the economic, social and physical areas but extended to include ideological manipulation which took - among many forms - a theological one, black Christians, pastors and theologians were called upon to respond theologically to counteract and restrict mental damage on Black Christians. They had to join hands with black sociologists, economists, psychologists and other scientists.

In the field of Black Theology it is evident that the selection of themes and determination of priorities was related to the historical development of objective conditions as well as the subjective state of the Christian faith of the oppressed. At no time did Black Theology follow the European and white American agenda because it was part of the problem. That would not have helped to build theological resistance against further corrosion of the mind of the oppressed. And as Steve Biko aptly put it 'the mind of the oppressed is the most potent weapon in the hands of the oppressor'. To deprive the oppressor of this precious mind Black theology had to determine its independent agenda which more often that not, contradicts that of most white theologians.

In the actual systematic development of Black theology two poles of reference stand out: the Exodus and the praxis of Jesus, the Messiah (Christology). Much of the earlier black theology revolves around them as events that provide a powerful paradigm of liberation. In both cases the notion of history which is generally insufficiently dealt with, if not totally neglected, by traditional white theology, is regarded as most important. A historical approach to these events brings out their dynamic theological character. All the different theological concepts which are dealt with - creation, liberation, justice, reconciliation and so on are defrozen and injected with a dose of historicity by a people for whom history and time had stood still until they decided to move them. Black people have been awakened to regard 'the world as history in the making' and themselves as active participants in its making and moulding. To them history is not simply harmonious but conflictual as well, because of inherent contradictions and antagonism among blacks and whites. It is dialectical and stumbles through moments of harmony and conflict in its forward movement. In opposition to a notion of history which moves independently of the human agency, with God alone in action, a notion that creates passivity among the oppressed who cannot wait an extra day longer for change, black theologians emphasize black people's agency as co-workers with God. They work with God in the historical destruction of structures, institutions and attitudes that make acquisition of life and dignity by black people impossible. Black Christians - men and women, young and old- are shown, biblically, that they should be on the cutting edge of the struggle to create new structures and institutions which they can use to gain economic justice, social equality and political empowerment as a people and as individuals. It is their Christian vocation to do this in anticipation of the coming of the Kingdom of God. To stimulate this active discipleship Black Theology emphasizes people's God-given potency for revolutionary action and encourage black people to believe in themselves as well as in their abilities to define, shape and reshape their world and social relationships. It is in connection with these emphases that Allan Boesak discussed the biblical basis of black power in the middle 1970s and Simon Maimela does today in the middle of the 1980s. (As things are today in South Africa, this notion of black power in various forms - its channelling, direction and utilization will continue to be emphasized by Black theology.) An understanding of the central position and role of the modern racist state in organizing and utilizing power to foster injustice and violently resist all efforts towards peace makes these emphases imperative.

In this area Cone and Albert Cleage have remained loyal to the earliest positions of black consciousness and black power. When Cone enters dialogue with black marxists he does so without abandoning that position which deals so aptly with racism. He complements it with a paradigm that is capable of dealing better with capitalism. In that way he is strengthened instead of weakened. Charles West is open to criticism in this area.[24] For him racism is only responsible for the extra suffering of black people and not for their basic suffering. The tragedy with many black South African theologians and activists is that in a situation in which racism is still rampant and promises to be more so as the struggle heats up they have dumped Black Consciousness in favour of the more attractive and fashionable orthodox marxian paradigm. They believe that it is more adequate in dealing with both racism and capitalism in spite of the absence of evidence supporting that claim. These groups can learn from the American experience that these two paradigms complement each other and become more open in their dialogue with fellow theologians of the former persuasion.

Black Theology also deals at length, as it is evident in the writings of the period around the 1976 Soweto uprisings, with the experience of suffering and death both within the Exodus journey as well as in Christology as the major fountain head of the Christian faith. Since 1976 the cross continues to hang heavily over black South Africa. Institutional resistance (sin) which violently confronts all followers of the radical prophets and Jesus the black Messiah in the Exodus of black people results in inconceivable suffering and genocidal killing of our people all over our country. Their suffering, through heinous forms of torture, shootings and callous rape of our school children, is related to the suffering of Jesus and his death at the hands of the state that acted in the name of the economically, politically and religiously powerful. As early as 1974 the endless killing of so many young people before their time, let alone the invisible internal bleeding of millions of our people as a result of economic and psychological torture, already constituted a crucial theological problem for M. Buthelezi. Dying in the path of a radical discipleship was made even more of a problem because there was then no visible convincing sign that the wall of apartheid was cracking. Instead it was toughening and thickening day by day, making it imperative for theology to descend deeper and deeper into the dark mysteries of the suffering and death of Jesus in its search for the presence of God and his promises for our people. Black theology cannot but continue to search for the christological meaning of the suffering and death of our people because their innocent blood continues to scream to God for justice like the blood of Abel. Within the South African valley of death of innocent black children who try to do God's will by following in the footsteps of Jesus the Messiah, Black Theology is bound to stand with both feet. It will have to explore seriously, in this overshadowing atmosphere of death and despair, a new and meaningful way of understanding and articulating the faith of a resurrection that denies death a word of finality in the world. Black Theology owes this to the black departed, the black living and the black unborn whose history is characterized by death and the absence of God. The power of resurrection which is produced from the tomb of Jesus is desperately needed to break the umbilical cord of racist oppression that binds black people to the South African flaming pyre.

BIBLIOGRAPHY

1. S Biko Statement made in court during the SASO-BPC trial as quoted by A. Millard. See his *'Testimony of Steve Biko'* (New York: Panther Books, Granada Publishing, 1979) p.94
2. B Goba 'Doing Theology in South Africa: *A Black Christian Perspective'* in *Journal of Theology for Southern Africa,* June 1980, p25ff
3. I J Mosala 'The use of the Bible in Black Theology' in I J Mosala and B Tlhagale *(eds):The Unquestionable* Right *to be Free'*(Skotaville, Johannesburg,1986)p175ff
4. See D Bosch 'Currents and crosscurrents in South African *Black Theology'* in G S Wilmore and J H Cone (eds.): *Black Theology, a Docu*mentary History, 1966-1979, (New York,Orbis Books, 1979) p233 ff
5. See G S Wilmore's *Black Religion and Black Radicalism* (New York, Anchor Books 1973) p 295f. Also see Cone's *God of the Oppressed* (Seabury Press, New York, 1975), p252f; also see Cone's *My Soul Looks Back* (Abingdon, Nashville, 1982) p82
6. See Mokgethi Motlhabi (ed.): *Essays on Black Theology,*(Johannesburg: UCM. 1972).
7. See B Tlhagale's "Towards a Black Theology of Labour" in C.Villa-Vicencio and J W De Gruchy (eds): *Resistance and Hope (David Ph*ilip:Cape Town,1985) p126ff.
8. See C West: *Prophesy Deliverance*: Westminster Press, Philadelphia, 1982, Cone's *My Soul looks back;* also see Frances *Beale's' Dou*ble *Jeopardy:To be Black and Female'* in *Black Theology*: A Documentary History.
9. Sergio Torres and John Eagleson (eds.):*The Challenge of Basic Christian Communities*-New York, Maryknoll, Orbis Books,1981.
10. See especially Cornel West's paper in *The Challenge of Basic Christian Communities*. Also see Cone's arguments in *My Soul Looks Back* as well as in *For my people.*
11. I J Mosala's 'African Independent Churches: a study in soci*o*-theological protest' *in Resistance and Hope*.

12. Bernadette Mosala's 'Black Theology and the Struggle of the Black Woman in South Africa' in *The Unquestionable Right to be Free* is along these lines.
13. See the articles by Frances Beale, Jacqueline Grant, Theresa Hoover, Pauli Murray and Alice Walker in *Black Theology: A Documentary History*.
14. Mosala's article entitled 'The use of the Bible in Black Theology' in *The Unquestionable right to be free* addresses this issue.
15. See TA Mofokeng: The *Crucified among the Crossbearers:Towards a Black Christology*-(Kampen, J.H. Kok, 1983)and A. A. Boesak : *Farewell to Innocence (Kampen,* J.H. Kok, 1976)
16. See J Deotis Roberts *'Liberation and Reconciliation-*(Westminster Press, Philadelphia*)* and Cone in his *A Black Theology of Liberation* (New York, J B Lippincott, 1970)
17. See Mosala's *'The Use of the Bible in Black Theology,'* Cone's *God of the Oppressed* and also J Deotis Roberts'- *Roots of a Black Future: Family and Church* (The Westminster Press, Philadelphia,1980).
18. See G S Wilmore's *Black Religion and Black Radicalism.*
19. See *Farewell to Innocence* for Boesak's position and *Essays on Black Theology* for that of M Buthelezi. S Biko's position on this issue comes out clearly in his 'Black Consciousness and the quest for true humanity' in *Essays on Black Theology.*
20. See Hans-Jurgen Becken(ed): *Relevant Theology for Africa-*(Durban, Lutheran Pub. House, 1973.
21. S S Maimela: 'Salvation in African Traditional Religions' in *Missionalia* Vol.13, No2, August 1985.
22. See I J Mosala The Relevance of African Traditional Religions and their relevance to Black Theology' in *The Unquestionable right to be Free.*
23. See Sergio Torres and Kofi Appiah-Kubi (eds.): *African Theology en Route* (Maryknoll, New York: Orbis Books, 1979).

24. See Cone's *A Black Theology of Liberation* and Cornel West's *Prophesy Deliverance.*
25. See C West's *Prophesy Deliverance.*

9

The Future and Mutual Support: Zama Asefani

Josiah U. Young

Introduction

My purpose in this essay is to reflect on our future which is the promise of penultimate liberation. But I want to first explain the Zulu words in the title of this essay and why I chose them. And then I will explain in more detail the way in which I will reflect on the future of our theologies.

'*Zama Asefani*' means 'the promise of a future'. Roughly translated '*zama asefani*' means 'try, things will be different'. I came across the imperative statement in the winter of 1982 while in KwaZulu, South Africa. I still clearly remember the deprivation of the images of the people and the desolation of that part of the Zulu homeland. Africans were living on rocks in an arid, dusty, seemingly God-forsaken place. They were desperately eeking out a minimal subsistence, trying heroically to keep some vestige of the dignity of the sacred ground of their ancestors. In the midst of that deprivation, a young man approached me with a beaded breast plate on which are inscribed the words '*zama asefani*'. He sold it to me for one rand. 'What do the words mean?', I asked. My translator explained, 'it's something like 'if you don't succeed, try again'; no, better you should say, 'try, things will be different''.

Despite the poverty of the homelands, notwithstanding the unscrupulous manipulation of black labor, the influx control, the domestication devastation of African families, things will be different. We have hope in things unseen. *Zama asefani* is a heroic message. Back home in the States, travelling through Harlem, looking at the similarity between black suffering there and in Soweto, I was inspired by the words. They succinctly signify the relationship between life threatening struggle and hope. They convey the meaning of our joint struggles against a white supremacist ideology which translates into a ruthless capitalist practice, a praxis of exploitative oppression.

The breastplate is, for me, a symbol of our beginnings in God, nurturing in Christ, and future in the Spirit who enables us to struggle. We are empowered to try to change things because we know that we have been made in the image of God who means freedom. No oppressor, then, can deny us our natural birthright. Things will be different because the liberating meaning of the *imago dei* has been restored to us in Christ. As Jesus Christ perfects, in the Spirit, the image of God in human kind, we are bound to struggle for the liberation of the oppressed. This is to say, if God takes on the full humanity of the oppressed by suffering, dying and rising as the Oppressed One, then the Oppressed One has taken on the identity of our folk in the homelands and ghettos. God is with the oppressed. The indicative statement has a soteriological meaning indispensible for an understanding of a praxis of sanctification.

As we are moved to believe that our oppression contradicts grace and liberation, we are justified. As we become instruments which change contexts of oppression into contexts of liberation, we are made holy. Our future victory is incarnate in our faith. And when we and the Spirit account for the hope within us, the power of that promise is revealed in a praxis of liberation. Doing black theology means that faith without works is dead. Yes, we have work to do in the present which is intrinsic to the redemptive future. I reiterate then that my purpose here is to reflect on the future which is the promise of liberation. Indispensible for this reflection is a discussion of theological dimensions of our past and present. Only hindsight into the justified past and insight into our sanctified present will enable us to speak foresightedly of our redemptive future. Therefore, my paper is divided into three sections: on the past, the present and the future.

The Way of the Ancestors; Woza Dwane, Woza Turner

We come together out of an awareness of a historical relationship between blacks of South Africa and the United States. Bound together by links stronger than those that bind Afro-Americans to other Africans, chained together to the institutional anchors of white supremacy for at least three hundred years, we know the misery in dragging the weight of capitalism. Too well known to us is the ruthless segregation designed to give our oppressors economic advantage, comforts and privileges. How can we then in the name of God help to destroy apartheid and significantly curtail black socio-economic suffering in the United States so that our children will not in the future continue to die in adolescence?

The crises we face differ from the ones that brought bishop Henry McNeil Turner and Rev. Dwane together. But we certainly represent a continuum of their particular pan-African solidarity. Like David Walker, their ancestor in theological revolt, Turner and Dwane believed that God will not suffer us always to be oppressed. Our suffering will come to an end, in spite of all of the oppressors on this side of eternity. To ignore our ancestors is to invite theological imbalance. Their views anchor us to a tradition of theological pan-Africanism. Our ancestors in struggle tell us: try, things will be different. In other words, the legacies of our religious past help us to articulate the nature of our God today and envision our life in God tomorrow. Our ancestors such as Nat Turner, Theopholis Gold Stewart, and Enoch Mgijima found great meaning in the image of Christ descending with a double-edge tongue of retribution.

Nat Turner put it this way:

> *I heard a loud voice in the heavens and the spirit instantly appeared to me and said the serpent was loosened. And Christ had lain down the ilk he had born for the sins of men and that I should take it on and fight against the serpent for the time was fast approaching when the first should be last and the last should be first.*

When the horrified Mr. Gray, who listened to the confession of Nat Turner, asked Nat, 'do you not find yourself mistaken now?' A committed Turner replied, 'was not Christ crucified?' His remark reveals his faith in God's partiality to the oppressed; that God stands against the evils of white supremacy as surely as Jesus rose from the dead. He took seriously the promise that his savior would come to right the injustice of slavery.

The African Methodist Episcopal (AME) theologian Steward believed that the forces of light and darkness would not only square off in the United States, but in the international arena as well. Perceiving the dawning of World War I, Stewart thought the global conflict would result in the collapse of the western civilization. As David Wills explains, Stewart believed he foresaw the liberation of the other races and the beginnings of a new age in which Christ would reign. According to Stewart:

> *the white races of the earth have modified the Christian idea to an alarming idea by the Klan principle. So that it has become a white man's religion and is so recognized by the darker races.*

In the millennium, Stewart believed that Christianity would undergo its last penultimate reformation in order that 'the Christ may be all in all'.

In 1918, the South African Enoch Mgijima, influenced by the message of John Chilembwe's revolt in Nyasaland, preached of his visions. One of these visions represented a battle between two white governments. In his vision, he had seen a baboon crush these governments and destroy them. The Boers and the British were the governments and the baboon was an indigenous exemplar of black power. Mgijima's followers identified themselves with the Hebrew children of Exodus and fully expected their deliverance from Anglo-Boer rule. His apocalyptic interpretation of the Exodus led to a confrontation between his followers and the authorities.

In Mgijima, Steward and Turner, we see an inspired conviction in the righteousness of God and an unconditional identification of white supremacists with the anti-Christ. We also see their implicit assertion that we have a future beyond the destruction of apartheid and racism in the United States. Although some of us might find apocalyptical signs too mythical, we cannot fail to appreciate the righteousness of our ancestors' theological interpretation of the apocalypse. Revealed again is our historic conviction that God is with us in the battle against the princes of iniquity. We need not completely dismiss our ancestors' understanding of the revelation of John as uncritical credulous acceptances of archaic mythological idioms. On the contrary, myths tell us the truth of our perceptions of what is ultimately valuable. God hears the cries of his oppressed people and will intervene on their behalf against Babylon which aptly signifies the imperial west and South Africa.

The Already

In the United States, we stand at a new nadir in our history despite the blood of the martyrs of the Civil Rights Movement. Legislation passed and modest reparations enacted as a result of the agitation of the 1960s are significant but not nearly adequate. White supremacy is still a powerful frustrating force, tolerant of only a minority of blacks who are, for one reason or the other, provisionally palatable to white supremacist taste. Clearly the majority are forced to wrestle with the problem of being passed over or eased out or left out. The ascent of the era of Ronald Reagan has been precisely the descent of the era of Martin Luther King, Jr. Forces behind Reagan (e.g., the new right, the religious right, the neo-conservatives) have had a devastating effect on black North America. Their ascendancy must be analyzed in the face of the weakness of mainline black organizations and the removal of outstanding black leaders like Malcolm X and Martin King.

A matter of public record is the ruthless monitoring of mainline organizations by federal agencies. The government, under cover, retarded the advances of the 1960s. Now in the 1980s, there is a desperate need to revive in fresh ways the confrontational matrix which produces change. Indeed the black underclass still suffer gross deprivation that fueled the rage of the riots of the 1960s. Talk of affirmative action is meaningless to the black underclass. The anxiety and insecurity of the black professional are luxuries to them. Trapped in the violence of the ghetto, they are being crushed behind the wall of the systemic violence of white supremacy. The promised land has proven to be but an extension of Egypt's land. And the barriers that have historically held the black poor in cycles of despair have ossified. The suffering has been devastating. Neither the abortive anti-poverty programs nor the routinized bureaucracy of social aid have effectively mitigated the tragedy of the lives of the black poor.

For instance, in places like New York City's Harlem, we witness the third generation of the black underclass. Each generation sinks lower into the swamp of poverty which has made a mockery of family life and community wholesomeness. Domestic instability, pathetic institutional weakness and community chaos have led to a burgeoning inferno. And such a hell our young people are consuming. They either become kindling for the furnaces of our prisons, demonic apparitions haunting street corners and alleys or infantile parents, equipped only to perpetuate the American nightmare that haunted the vision of Malcolm X.

Yes, we are no longer lynched with impunity. Jim Crow is no longer legally practiced in the United States. Blacks are enfranchised and a very few run for president and head multinational corporations. I am not saying that that is necessarily good. But some people would point to that as a sign of progress. But white supremacy and exploitation of blacks continue and God, it seems to me, is not pleased.

In South Africa, it is still a case of the ballot or the bullet. The forces of darkness are still controlling the black majority with all the ruthless intensity of the anti-Christ. US foreign policy in southern Africa has for too long retarded the ascendancy of justice, particularly in South Africa. South Africa, as we all know, is indispensible for imperial investment and is a western ally in the cold war. Covert US action helps South Africa to destabilize frontline states. Destabilization is carried out by the South African defence force and its satellites, the Union for the Total Liberation of Angola (UNITA) and the Movement for National Resistance (MNR). White is still over black in southern Africa, exploding black dreams of development in order to preserve white hegemony over the means of production and the matrix of technological comforts. There is no justice in South Africa. And God stands against her in apocalyptic fashion.

Current divestment policies and sanctions against South Africa are steps in the right direction. Certainly investment never really facilitated non-violent reform. It was believed that black laborers would gain by sheer force of numbers the bargaining power to influence an essentially disinterested capitalist infrastructure. Insofar as the infrastructure upholds the settlers, it is not disinterested. Insofar as investment allows the Republic to dictate the internal policy, it upholds apartheid, the disfranchisement of the majority, the polarization and the political economy by way of township and homeland.

The western capitalist, who claim that homeland leadership will be the channel of reform, loose sight of how that leadership has complicity in the maintenance of a vicious system of deprivation and exploitation. The same contradiction is found in the urban townships. South Africa's futile attempt to create a buffer class to mitigate the outrage of the black majority and show to the global community a veneer of reform serves only to intensify conflict. Blacks are still locked into the debilitating matrix of apartheid. They are harassed, exploited, tortured and murdered. But the South African people are strong and their leadership is sure.

Not to be missed in this scenario is the character of Afrikaner, white supremacist intransigence to change. Their ungodly use of the neo-Calvinistic notion of predestination leads them to legitimate their demonic behavior in theologies which profane the meaning of the Exodus. Ironically and tragically they identify with the Hebrew children, identifying the Canaanites with the so-called bantu. They believe with fanatical self-righteousness that South Africa is the land given to them by God. Losing sight of the meaning of the association of the Old and the New testaments, they fail to see Exodus with the fresh paradigmatic, christological insights of liberation theologians. More specifically, Exodus works theologically for Christians today only when used by the oppressed who proclaim that the God who swallowed Pharaoh becomes one of the progeny of the slaves who crossed over into Canaan. The meaning then of the association between the Exodus and the gospel is uncovered in the incarnation which means today that Christ is found in the dust and smoke of Soweto. One cannot appeal to the Exodus in Christian terms without being in solidarity with the oppressed. Afrikaners who claim to be elect suffer from a critical case of hardening of the heart. May the spirit soften their hearts causing them to repent of their mortal sins. If not, to take a bit from Revelation, that the evil doers still do evil and the filthy still be filthy and the righteous still do right and the holy still be holy. It is midnight in South Africa. Time is running out.

The Not Yet

Our future will mean little until we in God's providence are made agents of black power in the United States and the destruction of apartheid in South Africa. The meaning of our ancestors' assimilation of apocalyptic imagery should not be lost on us or to us. Across the board, blacks are held down, held back, and set back. We black theologians then must have a vision of the future which is inextricable from a praxis of the present. If we are to have any future to speak of, we must seek right now the liberation of our folk by any means necessary. Determination of the means necessary to effect substantive change will not emerge from anger misdirected toward violence.

However, by any means necessary does not mean violence necessarily. Indeed in the United States, I am committed to non-violence because it appears to be, at this time, the best means of change. This is especially the case given the legacy of Martin King whose radical praxis of non-violence, though rusted now from disuse, could have brought the status-quo to its knees. In the United States, by any means necessary signifies critical study of the failure of the last twenty years. Beloved community must mean first black solidarity. Commitment to ethnic solidarity and the principle of do-for-self is proportional to the extent which we refuse to co-operate with or be co-opted by Pharoah.

We still need to write, in the tradition of James Cone, theologies of black power. Far from being dated, Cone's analysis of the theological compatibility of the gospel and black power is the best paradigm for producing Christian meaning from our current pathetic state. In the United States we need to create alternative strategies independent of two party politics. If we black Americans then are to have integrity in the eyes of our black South African siblings, we must struggle for social, economic power within the context of our own communities in a way that refuses to bargain with the devil.

In South Africa, we must be aware of the history of liberation struggles in southern Africa. Broken flesh and bloodshed there have been redemptive insofar as authentic liberation armies have cut short the reign of the anti-Christ. Let us hope that the future liberation in store for blacks in South Africa will be achieved by the plagues of strikes. Let us hope that strikes will be the means whereby Pharoah will be forced to let go. But if revolution is the way to the future, then even so come Lord Jesus. I am aware of how easy it is for me to talk in positive terms of armed struggle in South Africa. Living a somewhat privileged life in Afro-America, I am hardly prey to the consequences of violent struggle in South Africa today. Nonetheless, I am compelled to support the freedom fighters. Having said that, I refuse to allow the issue of violence to be used as a foil mitigating the fact that apartheid is a mortal sin. I am not by any stretch of the imagination advocating violence. Who can be an advocate of violence with the dead of Soweto still vividly in mind? My prayer is that the Republic and its western beasts will repent of their sins and abandon their intransigent iniquity. Too many lives have been lost. Too many children have died for one to advocate violence in a way that is cavalier. But David slew Goliath and I believe that God will slay the Republic of South Africa. I believed God backed the struggle against the Nazis. And I believe God backs the liberation struggle in South Africa.

We then cannot fail to theologically consider the issues which devout Christians like Oliver Tambo and Nelson Mandela raise. Considering their voices, we cannot ignore the Old Testament witness to God's sanctification of violence, a sanctification neither hostile to peace, nor amoral but intrinsic to the historical process of redemption. But the Old Testament is insufficient by itself for a Christian understanding of salvation. I would like to consider the Old Testament as preparation for the incarnation.

Indeed the dynamic crisis of the present in South Africa impels us in faith to reflect on the role of the freedom fighters. To what extent will the guerrillas determine the future? What does Christ and the Spirit call us to do now? How are we called to assume the cross of discipleship and the proclamation of the liberation of the oppressed? How are we called to participate in the liberation of the oppressed and proclaim the acceptable year of the Lord? How must we in South Africa be faithful to our Lord in the face of the anti-Christ? What does Jesus want us to do now in order to be about a future of justice?

Prior to his ascension, we read about a Jesus who appears to be a non-violent teacher. In him is revealed the creative love of God. In him the human and the divine are perfectly reconciled. Healing the breach of alienation, Jesus overcomes death, securing for us a promise of ineffable longevity in God. Not by the sword did God conquer our sickness unto death. But by raising love from suffering and death, was death overcome. Clearly, (I should not say clearly) maybe the historical Jesus was a passivist and certain Christians rightly see him as an archetype of passivism. But this is only part of the story. The Son of Man of Revelation is a militant Christ who speaks with a double-edged truth of grace and judgement. Grace is intrinsic to judgement. Grace will continue to operate that way until we stop nailing one another to the forbidden tree of in-humanity; till we lift Desmond Tutu over P W Botha; till we lift peace over fascism and torture. Even so, the Christ of Revelation is coming to stop the anti-Christ, not by non-violent suffering but by the power of the armies of heaven. The particularities of our theological histories teach us that here is an important clue for finding theological meaning in revolutionary situations. We are forced to explore new meanings of Christian realism, realizing the theological support of revolution is a distinct possibility. We Afro-American theologians must be willing to pull out all stops in support of such a possibility. It is a possibility as real as tomorrow.

If we believe our destinies are linked, then we must live out the truth of that conviction now. The already is the not yet. We must believe today that tomorrow the triumph of one-person-one-vote in South Africa will translate into the triumph of black power in Afro-America. If we are pan-African siblings, then we must start now to forge a steel bond of love and commitment to one another. If indeed the triumph of the freedom struggle in South Africa and the fruition of black power are analogous to the love of God, then nothing can separate us from each other and from the love of God.

Nonetheless the problems we face are formidable. In the United States, the problem of the proliferation of the black underclass and the political impotency of the black middle class in leading the black poor will not be solved by black power rhetoric alone. South Africa's awesome military machine, the weakness of the frontline states, and the unholy alliance between the west and the Anglo-Boer regime make one think of the terrific odds against liberation. Even when the people win in South Africa, the problem of the diversity of interests already at work threatens to cripple the development of a stable political economy. Already the problems of ethnicity deeply embedded in ancestral history and tragically heightened by the coming of the white man threaten the liberation struggle.

After independence, ethnic conflict may be further manipulated by ideological enmity among liberation groups and between class interests. It is a pattern endemic to the African continent: the thorn in the side of efforts to effect international unity within the continent, the cancer which blocks national development, the achilles heel of so-called independence to which the arrows of neo-imperialism fly with devastating accuracy. But I reiterate that in faith nothing will separate us from the love of God. If we truly learn to love one another, bearing all things, hoping all things, things will be different. Faith in our liberation, confidence that we have a future unburdened by white supremacy is not a foolish hope. After all we hope in things unseen. If we try in the Spirit, things will be different.

The extent to which blacks love blacks in Africa and in Afro-America is proportionate to the extent to which black theologies of liberation will take on new meanings in the future. In other words, let us hope the theme of liberation in our theologies will mean tomorrow a pan-African solidarity which through a creative alliance of our churches, a pooling of economic resources, and a reciprocity in political interests will overcome among and between us a deadening praxis of division. We cannot afford to wander in the wilderness. If we are to go with God who destroys the institutions of white supremacy and economic exploitation, we must try to live lives that are perfect in love toward one another. Only then will things be different in a way redemptive for the world. Only then shall we live in the fulfillment of the promise that is the hope within us. *Zama Asefani*, brothers and sisters. Things will be different.

10

Prospects for the Future and Building of Alliances

Itumeleng J. Mosala

Two insights may provide useful starting points for an attempt to develop a vision of the future of black theology. Both of these are inscribed in Marx's celebrated political text, 'The Eighteenth Brumaire of Louis Bonaparte'. The one insight concerns the discursive weapons of struggle that activists in oppositional struggles invoke; and the other involves the qualitative difference that Marx observes between bourgeois and proletarian revolutions. About the first he writes:

> *M*en [sic] make their history, but they do not make it just as they please; they do not make it under circumstances chosen by themselves, but under circumstances directly found, given and transmitted from the past. The tradition of all the dead generations weighs like a nightmare on the brain of the living. And just when they seem engaged in revolutionising themselves and things, in creating something entirely new, precisely in such epochs of revolutionary crisis they anxiously conjure up the spirits of the past to their service and borrow from them names, battle slogans and costumes in order to present the new scene of world history in this time-honored disguise and this borrowed language... The awakening of the dead in those revolutions therefore served the purpose of glorifying new struggle, not of parodying the old; of magnifying the given tasks in imagination, not of taking flight from their solution in reality; of finding once more the spirit of revolution, not of making its ghost walk again...Earlier revolutions

required world-historical recollections in order to drug themselves concerning their own content. In order to arrive at its content, the revolution of the nineteenth century must let the dead bury the dead. There the phrase went beyond the content; here the content goes beyond the phrase.[1]

Concerning the second insight, Marx asserts:

Bourgeois revolutions, like those of the eighteenth century, storm more swiftly from success to success; their dramatic effects outdo each other; men and things seem set in sparkling brilliants; ecstasy is the everyday spirit; but they are short lived; soon they have attained their zenith, and a long depression lays hold of society before it learns soberly to assimilate the results of its storm and stress period. Proletarian revolutions, on the other hand, like those of the nineteenth century, criticize themselves consistently, interrupt themselves continually in their own course, come back to the apparently accomplished in order to begin it afresh, decide with unmerciful thoroughness the inadequacies, weaknesses and paltriness of their first attempts, seem to throw down their adversary only in order that he may draw new strength from the earth and rise again more gigantic before them...[2]

In America and South Africa, black theologians have done both of these two things. They have appealed to their history and culture for tools of self-defense and struggle. By doing this, they have affirmed the significance of Gayraud Wilmore's assertion that 'the first source of black theology is the black community itself'.[3] Similarly, albeit thinly and unsystematically, they have faced the question which J. Ngubane poses as *the* challenge of black theology: '...is it more comprehensive, concerned not only with oppressive societal issues, but also with cultural and philosophical issues?'[4]

Black theologians have taken their cue from the past traditions of struggle in order to stage a revolution in the *present*. The value of this has been to maintain a historical perspective without which present struggles retain a fatal blind spot. The concern remains, however, whether in this appropriation of history and culture the 'phrase goes beyond the content or the content beyond the phrase'.

But that is precisely the reason for this conference of Azanians and African Americans. We are here to criticize and interrupt ourselves; to return to our apparent successes in order to start again. We are gathered here to allow ourselves an unmerciful self-decision on our weaknesses and the paltriness of our first attempts. And even more fundamentally, we are here to remind ourselves that our adversary has fallen down only in order that he or she may draw new strength and rise again more gigantic than before. The recent re-emergence in South Africa of white liberalism under the guise of 'left progressivism' is a case in point.

Thus a consideration of the future prospects of black theology implies an appraisal of its projective, critical and appropriative functions.[5] This is necessary if black theology is not to degenerate into a theological fad. It is better to start again, in the spirit of Marx's second insight, than to pass quickly from one contentless revolution to another. Black theologians must make clear the nature of the society they struggle for. It is inadequate to get by their 'projective' responsibility by uncritically adopting the abstract values of western liberal democracy, like justice, peace, reconciliation and so on. Also, if black theologians are not to fall prey to the oppressive aspects of the dominant capitalist cultural discourses, they need autonomous critical apparatuses. This is especially indispensable in areas such as biblical hermeneutics. The reason is that here in particular theologians have been captive to the hermeneutical and exegetical assumptions of White Theology.[6] In addition, the question of how black theologians 'appropriate' received religious and cultural traditions is of vital importance. The future of black theology is as much dependent on its ability to create new practices as to utilize received discourses.

Assuming the validity of these points I have just made, four areas of concern immediately suggest themselves as requiring urgent critical activity.

1. Definitions

In the early days of black theology, the definitional task was taken very seriously. Black theology was defined as reflection on the black experience in the light of the "Word of God". Later this definition was qualified, especially in South Africa, by explaining that blackness here did not refer to the colour of the skin.[7] Since then there has been a shift in emphasis from definitions to the formulations of content and form within black theology.

Clearly, this shift to the actual 'doing' of black theology is to be welcomed. Mokgethi Motlhabi is certainly correct in insisting on the need for 'stage two' of Black Theology.[8] Nevertheless, an enormous price will be paid, when there is a complete abandonment of the definitional task. In order to appreciate this, let us look again at the implications of the definition of black theology in South Africa.

The initial definition of black theology implied that only black people could do black theology. In fact, in the early days there was no question that this was the case. At this point the black theological project was still inseparably tied to the black revolt against the totality of the white world. Neither black nor white people had any doubt about the nature of this revolt. As Black Theology sought accommodation within the discursive terrain controlled by the beneficiaries of the white world, however, problems arose. In the domain of academic activity where the ideology of liberalism provides the controlling metaphors, black theology needed to readjust in order to be accommodated. This was particularly serious in South Africa where the white world is *really* white. Liberal theologians had been grieved, while emerging black theologians, the latter being invariably the products of the former, were contradicted, by the demands of the black revolt and its consequences for black theology. Was it not the case that white liberal theologians had helped to create the mood, at least discursively, that led to the rise of black theology? But of course, as Mafeje argues, they did not understand the principle of negation.[9] And so black theologians came to their rescue; they qualified blackness to include those white people who are supposedly black in thinking.

Since then Black Theology has had nothing but trouble in South Africa, with white people virtually silencing it in favor of Latin American liberation theology. This debate needs to be aggressively revisited. What, for instance, is the difference between contextual theology and Black Theology in South Africa? Is there an ideological-cultural explanation of white 'progressive' theologians predilection for Latin American Liberation Theology?

But, of course, there was a fundamental weakness in black theology which made the onslaught on it possible. This weakness has to do with our failure to do 'internal' definitional work. If in the beginning it was clear that white people could not do black theology, did it follow, though, that all black people could do black theology? Was it correct to be so loose in our definition of the black theological practice as to imply that it amounted to any theology done by any group of black people? The need to tighten up the theoretical and ideological screws in this area cannot be overemphasized. This applies equally to the USA and South African situations.

I argue for an ongoing concern for the definitional task of Black Theology for two reasons. First, because this task is inseparable from the equally important responsibility to 'do' black theology. The function of naming reality is an integral part of the process of creating that reality. We name and rename as we execute the production of the black theological discourses. And this terrain is not an ideologically neutral one. The very existence of Black Theology bears witness to the fact that the definitional function of theological practice is a site of fierce class, gender and cultural struggles.

Second, and tied up with the first reason, the definitional task is crucial to the ongoing practice of black theology because of the present historical conjuncture: the era of monopoly capitalism. This is the period of capitalist development when the 'commodity form' extends its influence to all aspects of human life. It is the period of the Universal Market. In this period all discourses, status quo-oriented ones as well as oppositional ones, are vulnerable to co-optation by the 'commodity form'. Thus in this conjuncture, the question of the 'images of struggle' always calls to mind its dialectical counterpart, the 'struggle for images'.[11] In the area of Black Theology this issue is of pivotal significance. For here, as anywhere, Marx's words ring true that 'In every epoch, the ruling ideas are the ideas of the ruling class'[12.] What needs to be added, though, is that in no epoch are the ruling ideas uncontested. The discursive sphere of society is as much an arena of struggle as the non-discursive sphere.

The danger, however, of 'neo-Young-Hegelianism' must be avoided. The definitional task, and the struggle for images which goes with it, is not a matter of abstract rearrangement of furniture. On the contrary, genuine liberative definitional work requires concrete involvement in actual historical struggles. This task should not be seen as an alternative to 'fighting in the streets or in the mountains'.[13] Rather, it is an integral part of the same process.

I must underline this point of the writing of theory and practice. For indeed that is what the 'definitional task' is in fact about. Presently it defines the nature of the crisis of black politics as was illustrated by the Tottenham uprisings in England and the KTC/Cross Roads fiasco in South Africa recently. For as Stuart Hall so poignantly articulated in relation to the Tottemhan problem:

> 'Keeping faith with the people who, in the teeth of relentless oppression, spontaneously resist, is alright on the night. But it is not enough when the next day dawns, since all it means is that, sooner or later, the front line troops, with their superior weapons and sophisticated responses, will corner some of our young people on some dark night along one of these walkways and take their revenge on Tottenham.'[14]

The ongoing task of defining Black Theology, therefore, must not be separated from the continuing production process of the black theological discourses of liberation. Cornel West's *Prophesy Deliverance,* Takatso Mofokeng's *The Crucified Among The Crossbearers:,* James Cone's *For My People*: and the Azanian production, *The Unquestionable Right to be Free*, should all afford us a moment to pause and ask, what after sixteen years do we mean by Black Theology?

2. Black Feminist Theology

The area of Black Feminist Theology presents one of the biggest challenges to black theologians. This is not because there is any doubt as to its importance. On the contrary, precisely because (as commonly held in revolutionary circles), the measure of the success of any liberation struggle is the extent of the liberation of women in that struggle.

Even more importantly, the problem of the "struggle between struggles" makes the question of a black feminist theology exceedingly urgent. The tendency by some struggles to want to subsume other struggles under their aegis is a characteristic feature of "discourse imperialism" under monopoly capitalism. The experience of women and blacks in supposedly socialist organizations is salutary in this regard.

Thus, not only is an autonomous black feminist theological discourse a necessity of the objective and subjective conditions of black women's struggle, it is also a condition for the successful execution of the black liberation struggle. Without such an autonomous discourse of struggle Black Theology is dangerously attenuated.

In this area, a sharing of resources between Azanians and African Americans could help correct the deficit and drag Black Theology out of a backwardness which only reinforces white cultural hegemony. A moratorium on other areas of black theological study and production may not be out of place at this time. This is particularly significant given the further super-exploitability of black women under conditions of monopoly capitalism.

3. Methodological Frameworks and Racism

So far an area of dependency, and in many ways neocolonialism, for black theology is that of methodological frameworks. Almost invariably we have been independent on the nature of our theological project but dependent on the discursive tools by which we carried it out. This was true of the radical liberal critique of racial imperialism as well as the recent class analysis of capitalist society and culture, both which underscored our methodological resistance of oppression.

In and of themselves, the methodological and theoretical frameworks borrowed from other social and historical *praxes* are not wrong. However the dangers do exist, that they may become the means by which new forms of cultural and racial chauvinism and domination could be inaugurated.

In the contemporary South African political discourse, for instance, this is an area in which some black oppositional practices have been debilitated by the white theoretical and epistemological paternalism. White people's privileged 'ideological-methodological' competence in this area has been, more than anything, the sole legitimator of their inclusion in the progressive circles. In fact the emergence recently of an autonomous, politically legitimating, discourse known as 'progressiveness' is a function of this specifically white privileged domain of methodological competence. Of course, this 'competence' is itself the product of the privileged position of white people, especially in areas such as education.

I do not make this point in order to devalue the contribution of this kind of injection into the oppositional practices in South Africa. Indeed the change from liberal democratic and moral rhetoric to quasi-socialist terminology of struggle in the country should be credited to this infusion of 'progressive' methodological frameworks into the black struggle in recent times.

The question, however, of the racism of the left which is as equally evil as the racism of the right needs to be addressed by black theologians. In this regard, we can learn an enormous amount of lessons from the feminist movement. This latter movement has an experience of working within the so-called progressive organizations.[15]

4. Black Working Class Culture

The fourth area which black theology needs to address seriously and concerning which lessons from both sides of the Atlantic must be drawn is that of the black working class culture. The black churches in the USA and especially the African Independent churches in South Africa provide a wealth of resources in this regard. The black working class culture represents the framework within which black oppressed and exploited peoples either succumb to or revolt against the dominant economic, political, bureaucratic and cultural discourses of their societies. A systematic and critical exploration and appropriation of the black working class culture is indispensable in the future development of black theology. The following questions could provide a starting point in such a quest:

1. What is the nature of the structure of black existence that makes possible the super-exploitability of the black labor-power?
2. What conditions of social life are necessary in order to ensure the permanent availability of black people as an exploitable form of cheap labor?
3. How are the cultural practices of the black communities made vulnerable to exploitation by the imperialist cultural discourses of monopoly or settler capitalism (e.g., Soweto art; The Bill Cosby Show; Mr T; etc.).
4. In what ways are black people made participants in their own oppression through manipulations of their consciousness as well as by more overtly repressive mechanisms, and how can this be dealt with; and more importantly what is the role of the church, Christianity, the bible and some inherited reactionary black cultural-religious traditions?

Conclusion

I would like to end by reiterating what I think is the fundamental problem facing the black Christian religious wing of the opposition to oppression and exploitation. It is this: when white people first encountered black people, they had the bible or Christianity and the black people had the land; the white people and the black people prayed; after the prayer, the white people had the land and the black people had the bible and Christianity. Now the question is: black people have chosen to use the bible and Christianity to get the land back; but can they get the land back and keep the bible and Christianity?

FOOTNOTES

1. Marx and Engels, *Selected Works*, in one Volume, (Lawrence and Wishart: London, 1868), pp.96-98.
2. Ibid., p.99
3. G Wilmore, *Black Religion and Black Radicalism*, (Orbis Books: Maryknoll, 1983), p235
4. I J Mosala and B. Tlhagale (eds), *The Unquestionable Right To be Free*, (Orbis Books: Maryknoll, 1986), p.89
5. T Eagleton, *Walter Benjamin Or Towards A Revolutionary Criticism,* (Verso, London, 1981). p.113.
6. I J Mosala and B Tlhagale, op.cit. pp.175ff.
7. A Boesak, *Farewell to Innocence,* (Ravan Press: Johannesburg, 1977), p27
8. In I J Mosala and B Tlhagale, *op.cit.* pxii.
9. A Majafe, 'The problem of Anthropology in Historical Perspective: An inquiry into the Growth of the Social Sciences,' *Canadian Journal of African Studies,* 10, no.2 (1976), p.319.
10. The Kairos Document's silence on black people and on the theological discourses of black people, namely, Black Theology and African theology, should be viewed in this light.
11. B Hilton-Barker, 'Images of War, War of Images,' *'Vula!',* (June, 1986), passim.
12. Marx and Engels, *The German Ideology*, edited by C J Arthur, Lawrence and Wishart, (London, 1970), p.64.
13. A Majafe, *op.cit.* p.332.
14. S Hall, 'Cold Comfort Farm,' *New Socialist*, (November 1985), p.12.
15. For a helpful analysis, see Iris Young, 'Socialist Feminism and the limits of Dual Systems Theory,' *Radical Religion*, vol V, no.1 (1980), passim. Specifically relevant to Black theology here is James H Cone's neglected classic: *The Black Church and Marxism,* (Institute for Democratic Socialism: New York, 1980).

Epilogue and Prospect

Simon S Maimela

Introductory Remarks

As the essays in this volume make it abundantly clear, Black theology owes its origin to the unique experience of the people of colour, especially of the African descent, in North America and South Africa. In both places the people's blackness was taken and rationalized by the dominant white groups as giving them enough reason to subject Blacks to the life of pain, humiliation, degradation, exploitation and oppression. In both places there was conscious or unconscious belief in the superiority of all white people, a superiority which entitles them to a position of political and economic power, dominance and privilege in relation to Blacks, who were regarded as inherently inferior and doomed to servitude.

In North America white racial domination revolved around the history of slavery which had a shattering effect on the personality and self-respect of the black people. For after being captured through surprise raids on unsuspecting African villages, millions of the people of colour were taken and driven like animals, treated as beasts of toil, shipped across the seas, and stripped of their language and culture. As slaves they were confined to the fringe of society, made economically dependent on their white slave masters and denied justice, freedom or a share in the political, economic and cultural spheres of the American society.

In South Africa, Blacks were victims of white settler colonialism. Whites used their cultural, scientific, economic and military power to conquer and subjugate Africans, to rob them of their land, their gold, cattle as well as other material resources, thereby denying them their dignity, culture, and human rights in all spheres of life. Not only did white Christians colonize Blacks but in some cases also enslaved the people of African ancestry, the Khoikhoi. The same colonizers almost wiped out the San people (the so-called Bushmen) who were alleged to have been stealing cattle from white farmers. For over three hundred years, a succession of white governments have ensured that the suppression, exploitation and deprivation of the people of colour will continue.

In the light of this white racial domination and the fact that in both North America and South Africa people claim to be Christians, one would have expected the Church and its theologians to include, in their theological reflection, the concrete and every day hard experiences of black people who bore the brunt of racial injustice and oppression. Thus reflecting critically on how the oppressed and dominated black Christians try to live out their faith under socio-political systems that were designed by white politicians to deny Blacks their humanity and dignity, one would have expected the Church to be prophetic in its denunciation of white racial prejudices, injustice and oppression to which the people of colour were subjected. In so doing the Church would have been an effective instrument which God uses to teach white Christians, especially, that there was nothing wrong with the humanity of the oppressed Blacks as their white colonial masters would have them believe.

Regrettably, however, theology in both North America and South Africa has largely been done by white middle class theologians and some black priests who are comfortably situated in the society. The result is that in both North America and South Africa we have had colonial theologies which, wittingly or unwittingly, have taken a preferential option for the powerful in order to serve the socio-economic and political interests of white overlords. These theologies could justifiably be characterized as the enemy of the oppressed black people. For the distinguishing feature of these theologies lies in the fact that they teach an authoritarian God, who, as the Supreme Being in the universe, establishes racial classes in every society. Thus this God insists that there will always be the rich white people and poor black people in the society, because this colonial and capitalist God accepts poverty as part of the divine will for the underdogs, most particularly for the people of colour.

To ensure that this situation of unequal distribution of material resources remains unchanged, white theology has taught and continues to teach that the capitalist God has established law and order in every society in favour of white folks, and demands obedience to the authority of both the Church and state.[1] This attempted theological justification of the glaring unequal distribution of socio-political and economic rights and privileges between different classes in white dominated societies has led an astute politician, Napoleon, to remark rather perceptively about the ideological function of religion, when he writes:

> As far as I am concerned, I do not see in religion the mystery of the incarnation but the mystery of social order: it links the idea of inequality to heaven which prevents the rich person from being murdered by the poor...How can there be order in the state without religion? Society cannot exist without inequality of fortunes and the inequality of fortunes could not subsist without religion. Whenever a half-starved person is near another who is glutted, it is impossible to reconcile the difference if there is not an authority to say to him: 'God wills it so, it is necessary that there be rich and poor in the world, but afterwards in eternity there will be a different distribution'.[2]

Black theology must therefore be understood against this background of racial oppression as well as attempts by white theologians to justify white domination and their socio-political and economic privileges. For as it was the common practice during the modern European colonial period, the theological self-understanding of white people equated Christianity with white pursuit of their economic and socio-political interests. By teaching that white people were superior to black people, white theology made it possible for white Christians to plunder and exploit black labour and material resources without moral qualms. It did so simply by disregarding white political and economic domination as well as the oppression of the people of colour as relevant data for theological reflection. Hence theology could discuss the doctrine of God as the loving Creator and Saviour without correlating its understanding of God with the oppressive and destructive social institutions which subjected black people to various forms of humiliations.

Instead white theology emphasized the sharp separation between the bodily and spiritual needs of the oppressed black people. Hence white theology permitted the missionary fervour of saving 'individual souls' of the black folks and the continued white economic exploitation of the people of colour to exist side by side. Meanwhile both the white oppressor and the oppressed people of colour were taught that life on earth, especially for Blacks, was a preparation for the life hereafter. Thus refusing to focus attention on what is concretely wrong in the unequal socio-political and economic relationships, white theology did, and continues to, teach the oppressed Blacks about individualistic sins of the heart, the rottenness of human life on this side of the grave, and human helplessness in the face of sin — all of which make human brotherhood and sisterhood unrealizable on this side of the grave, even among those who call themselves Christians. Instead white theology taught that, because of the original sin, the social sins of human greed, domination, oppression and exploitation of human beings by their fellows are realities that the people of colour must learn to live with.

What Is Right With Black Theology?

Black theology, born out of the situation of oppression, is a theological protest against white racial domination. It is theology which aims at reflecting on the Black experience of oppression in the light of the gospel. As black Christians began to read the Bible in the light of their social experience in the so-called Christians countries of North America and South Africa, they discovered the contradiction between what the Bible proclaims and the message which their oppressors taught them. Thus beginning with their actual, concrete experiences of oppression and suffering caused by the dominant white oppressors who wield all the political, economic, judicial, cultural and theological power, oppressors who go to great lengths to use the Christian faith to retain that power, black Christians could not help but become aware that there is something wrong about the white Christian attempts to support the tragic marriage between the accepted white theology and the exploitative and unjust economic and political arrangements which threatened to dehumanize black Christians. Put somewhat differently, black Christians became suspicious not only about the situation of injustice and distorted theology which unashamedly gave support to the privileged status of white people, but also began the task of unmasking the reality of oppression and the ideological mechanisms (that is the total superstructure) that underpin and morally justify the social forces that foster and perpetrate the oppression of the people of colour. Furthermore, as Blacks began to relate their experiences of dehumanization to the biblical proclamation of the God of love, asking questions such as: Why did God create me black? Why does God allow white Christians to oppress black people, whom God also loves, simply because of their colour? What does God say and what is God willing to do about this situation of oppression? It began to dawn on believing Blacks that the reality of the politics of domination they see and experience differed from what they found in the Bible. For in the Bible God is not revealed as a category to be manipulated for the maintenance of the privileged status quo of white domination. Rather God is revealed there as the liberator God who battles against injustice and human misery in order to establish justice and right for the oppressed. Thus drawing their inspiration from a theological vision in which God is portrayed as the Liberator of slaves from the Egyptian captivity, black theologians began to reject the dominant white expressions of Christianity and to develop a Black Theology of liberation whose task, among others, was and remains that of confronting, questing and rejecting any vision of a god who fails to hear the cry of the poor and oppressed Blacks[3]. Inspired by the vision of this liberating God, Black Theology of liberation attempts to provide the struggling black people with an alternative biblical and theological models (visions) with which to both resist the extreme demands of white racial oppression and work for the liberation of the people of colour. In so doing, Black Theology empowers and encourages the black people to become subjects of their own history and destiny, thus assuming the role of being the agents of their own liberation as well as becoming the creators of just and humane social structures.

3. The Relevance And Contribution Of Black Theology

According to the biblical witness the human condition is structured in such a way that individuals find themselves living in a multiple network of relationships between God and human beings, between human beings themselves, and between humans and the rest of creation. Unfortunately these multiple relationships, necessary as they are for corporate life, mutual support and self-fulfillment, have been shattered and broken by sin. Sin is understood to have infested and distorted these relationships, thereby transforming the human condition into one of a radical estrangement, separation from God, from one another, and from the rest of creation. Therefore, when we look around at the world in which we live and at ourselves, the present reality of sin is made manifest in the life of individuals such as selfishness, lovelessness, and refusal to lend help to our human fellows, resulting in a broken world in which humans experience oppression and injustice, poverty and hunger.

The good news, according to the other side of the biblical message, is that God did not admit defeat in the face of sin. Instead, in the vicarious suffering and death of Jesus Christ on the cross and in his glorious resurrection, God procured an effective remedy for sin and its social consequences. Thus the Christ-event constitutes an atonement, that is, a healing or restoration of the broken relationships between God and humans and between human beings themselves. In consequence, the mission of the Church is one proclaiming God's victory over sin, a victory that aims at renewing and restoring these multiple networks of relationships not only between God and individuals believers but also between human beings themselves.

Now given the centrality which the Bible gives to the multiplicity of human relationships which sin has affected and broken, relationships which are restored when personal sins and guilt are forgiven, and when interpersonal animosities and hatred, that breed injustice and oppression, are overcome by the atoning work of Christ, one would have expected white theology to see the interconnection between the mission of the Church and the problem of racial oppression and exploitation of the people of colour. This is particularly so because oppression or exploitation of one human by another is not something natural but social in its origin: People oppress one another because humans beings in violation of God's will that they should love and serve one another, and in willful opposition to the reconciliation effected in Christ, subjugate, oppress and make others poor and dependent, by promoting unloving and unjust social relationships which sin has caused. In so doing sinful humans prevent the gospel from being experienced as a community-creating and life-giving event. In short, in white dominated societies white people oppress the people of colour because some white Christians, in pursuit of their narrow and selfish socio-political and economic interests, have deliberately decided to render God's reconciliation through the gospel ineffective.

Regrettably white theology, having allowed itself to be hijacked by the ruling class in order to legitimate the economic ambitions of white oppressors, chose to remain silent in the face of black oppression. It has failed to engage itself in actions that promote justice in society so that God's justice, reconciliation and peace promised by the gospel could also become experienced realities in the lives of the oppressed Blacks.

Many reasons could be advanced for the failure of white theology to make the intrinsic connection between the confession of faith and confession of as well as working for justice in racial societies. Part of the reason for that failure is the tendency to separate the dramatic stories of Genesis 3 and Genesis 4. As a result the sin that is discussed by much of white theology revolves around the sin of separation between God and human beings as portrayed in Genesis 3. Similarly, when white theology talks about salvation it talks primarily about the restoring of the broken vertical relationship between God and the individual sinners — thus giving the wrong impression that genuine salvation is possible apart from and in exclusion of the world in which individuals live. It does not take much reflection to see that white theology has committed a serious error here, in that part of the multiple relationships that constitute the Second Table of the Commandments was given less emphasis than the First Table. Yet when Jesus was asked: 'What is the great commandment in the law?' He flatly refused to be drawn into some kind of reductionism that restricts the law only to the human condition before the righteous God. Rather Jesus reminded his listeners that God's law has a two-fold dimension: The first is that we love the Lord our God with all our heart, soul and mind. The second, as important as the first, is to love our human fellows as ourselves.[4] Jesus was merely restating the summary of God's law as set out in the Torah.[5] God's law as summarized by Jesus thus intends to regulate the multiple networks of relationships into which all humans find themselves involved between God and humans, and between human beings themselves. In a very important sense, therefore, the summary of the law refers to the stories in Genesis 3 and Genesis 4 which, properly understood, should never be separated from one another but instead should be read together. The tendency in white theology to separate these stories has given white Christians the false impression that it is possible for individuals to be saved and yet continue to oppress black people. For white theology seems to suggest that it is possible for Whites to be saved and yet remain racist oppressors while at the same time remaining in good standing in the Church.[6]

In the light of this reductionism of white theology, which limits the application and relevance of the gospel to the so-called individual or spiritual sphere, where it is claimed that individuals could be saved in the midst of broken human relationships and socio-political injustices in which white oppressors allow the people of colour to waste away under the crushing burden of oppression and exploitation, I believe that Black Theology has a unique role to play by drawing some useful insights from the rich African anthropology. It is an open secret that black people even in North America where they have been cut off for centuries from the African culture and African Traditional Religions are, like their fellow Africans on the continent of Africa, characterized by their deep interest first and foremost in human relationships, an acute sense of justice and fair play. This is because they share that African anthropology which is human-centred and socially oriented. According to this anthropology, individuals are continually reminded that a fulfilling life cannot be had in isolation from their human fellows. Rather life is possible only in communal relationships in which individuals try to strike a balance between the private life and the social life, thus maintaining the network of relationships with their fellows so that every person is provided with a space to breathe and live a meaningful life. Accordingly, individuals were taught from early childhood ways and means of pursuing life in such a way that their actions would contribute toward the creation and nurturing of the network of multiple relationships to which I have referred to above between oneself and one's fellows, and ultimately between oneself and the spiritual world of ancestors and God. To maintain such a network of relationships, it was important to teach people to avoid bad relationships and to refrain from activities that are injurious to those relationships, actions that threaten to undermine the social fibre and stability of the community. Accordingly, individuals were socialized and expected to engage themselves in those social and personal activities that would enhance communal relationships, thus making life more humane and fulfilling for every person in the community. Allan Boesak concludes his book by describing this African anthropology thus:

> .. .it is possible to recapture what was sacred in the African community long before white people came — solidarity, respect for life, humanity, and community. It must be possible not only to recapture it, but to enhance it and bring it to full fruition in contemporary society. Genuine community lies beyond much struggle and despair, beyond reconciliation which will not come without conflict. It will come only through faith and courage. But again, this need be no other-wordly dream; it is as real as Africa itself. Indeed, *Motho ke motho ka batho babang.*

> This age-old African proverb has its equivalent in almost all African languages, and its meaning is still as profound as ever; even more: One is only human because of others, with others, for others.[7]

Furthermore, according to the African anthropology, sin and evil are believed to manifest themselves in the human attempt to destroy, to diminish and threaten the life of one's fellows. In consequence, any activity which aims at destroying or injuring our fellows is regarded as a serious evil or sin, because any such unloving act towards our fellow human beings is directed ultimately against God, the Creator and source of all life. Put somewhat differently, sin and evil in the African anthropology are measured in terms of the life of individuals who suffer injustice, oppression and destruction at the hands of their fellows. Sin is thus understood more in terms of the breach of loving relationships between human beings. Hence sin manifests itself in the lack of love in interpersonal relationships, through the state of absence of brotherhood and sisterhood. Sin is understood more in terms of the evil that people do to or perpetuate against one another than in terms of the human transgression of the divine law against the Godself. In other words, Africans do not think of sin and evil in terms of the legalistic structure through which human beings relate to God either by obeying or disobeying the Deity outside and beyond the social life in which individuals live as social selves. For this reason, Africans find themselves in full agreement with St. John when he writes:

> 'If anyone has material possessions and sees his brother in need but has no pity on him, how can the love of God be in him?' Dear children, let us not love in words or tongue but with actions and in truth.....No one has ever seen God; but if we love each other, God lives in us and his love is made complete in us...If anyone says, 'I love God,' yet hates his brother, he is a liar. For anyone who does not love his brother, whom he has seen, cannot love God, whom he has not seen...whoever loves God must also love his brother.[8]

It should be clear from the foregoing that the African anthropology looks at life holistically in terms of the multiple relationships in which life is lived. This African perspective on life which lays greater emphasis on the social wrongs and evils which human beings commit against one another is the one which Black Theology tries to lift up and offer as the African contribution to theological reflection on the great questions of sin and salvation. For it reminds the Church that sin is not only an evil activity which is directed against God but also has to do with all the evil deeds which are directed against their neighbours in the society. This African perspective concurs with the central biblical thrust which teaches that sin is both a vertical and horizontal reality, because in the final analysis it is not the Almighty, self-sufficient God who suffers at the hands of human exploiters, oppressors, and promoters of injustice in the world. Rather it is the human beings who suffer evil and oppression. However, because human beings suffer, God who is the Creator of all people is also offended by the deeds of those who perpetrate evil. In the African perspective, sin was thus correctly understood when it was seen to be committed and perpetrated through human activities that undermine all of life in the society such as witchcraft, evil spirit, hatred, evil-speaking against one's fellows and refusal to land help to those in need. For all these threaten to destroy what makes for life in society for all concerned. In order to overcome evil and sin in society, Africans spent enormous time and energy trying to ward off those evils. Even among those who have converted to Christianity some Africans continue to practice that are aimed at warding off evil continue. Hence, before a pastor baptizes a child, something has already been done by the traditional healers to fortify the life of the child against the evil forces that threaten it. Africans spend so much time finding out ways to protect individuals against evil both in this life and the next, because the focus is on the individual and his/her well being in communal relationships.

This African perspective on life is the heritage that Black Christians should bring to the Church, be it on the continent of Africa or in diaspora. In so doing Black theology will be reminding the Church that the stories of Genesis 3 and Genesis 4 should never be separated if Christians are to have a balanced, holistic theological understanding of sin and salvation. Indeed, Black Theology should insist that Genesis 4 which talks about the sin of individuals against their fellows in society is equally important as Genesis 3, because in the Christ-event God aimed at restoring both the vertical and horizontal relationships marred by sin and its social consequences.

By focusing on the network of relationships in which human beings find themselves, Black Theology is making a real theological contribution. It is reminding the Church that what stands at the centre of the Scripture and its message is not so much the fact that people are related to God through the law. Rather God in both the Old and the New Testaments is portrayed as the Creator who creates covenants of fellowship with God's people. Therefore, at the centre of the covenant is not law and its impossible demands which mortal humans cannot fulfil but life-giving relationships between God and human beings, relationships which make life possible. Hence Adam and Eve sinned not because they broke some lifeless law but because they undermined and eventually broke the life-giving relationships on which their life depended. And once this relationship was broken life could not continue as normal. Rather they had to suffer the consequence of the broken fellowship with their Creator: their friendship and cordial communication with God in the cool of the evening was abruptly terminated. Adam and Eve were, as a result, alienated from and began to blame each other. The story of Cain and Abel is but a continuation of the broken and alienated relationship between God and human beings, and between human beings themselves. Because sin is largely a matter of a breach of fellowship, Black Theology has a unique role to play, namely, one of helping the Church to make a decisive paradigm shift in the accepted theological focus from the legal structure to the network of multiple relationships in which human life is lived. In consequence, when any human act begins to disturb, threaten and undermine those relationships, Black Theology should challenge the Church to seriously begin to talk about sin on the horizontal level, a sin which ultimately is directed against God who created and continues to uphold those relationships.

This paradigm shift, emphasising on our understanding of sin leads to an important theological consequence: Black Theology should no longer borrow from the accepted stock of Western theological formulations that are not intelligible to the Black perspective on human life. The main casualty among these Western theological formulations will be the concept of 'justification by faith alone' which was propounded by Luther and others in order to give individual sinners the assurance of God's forgiveness and of life hereafter. This theological insight, however important and truthful it might be, should not be accepted by Black Theology without heavy qualifications. For the anxiety about individual salvation apart from and in exclusion of one's community and concern about the life hereafter — both of which are based on the legal structure that dominated Western thinking — are not African problems. For in the African anthropology individuals were assured of their future life because at death individuals were taken up and gathered to their ancestors. Here the salvation of the individual is not perceived to be a reality apart from and in exclusion of one's community. For this reason, any punishment for wrongdoing was something that was meted against the sinner on this side of the grave so that at death the sinner has already made things right with his or her fellow human beings, the ancestors and God. In the light of this, individuals did not have to face death with fear and trembling, agonising as to whether they would be saved or condemned to hell. Because this excessive brooding over the future and hell is not an African problem, Black Theology should discourage Christians, from making it the central concern and focus of Church ministry.

In conclusion, because for the people of African ancestry the focus in life is on the network of human interrelations, Black Theology should insist that the teaching of the Church should pay greater attention to what in the past were regarded in theological circles as venial as opposed to mortal sins. The focus thus should be on our continuing sinfulness between ourselves and our neigbours. Christians should focus on the wrongs they do to their fellows in society instead of focusing their gaze on the clouds in the sky, wondering about their future security in heaven. As Christians focus on those sinful activities which are hurtful to their neighbours, it will become possible for them to think of ways of overcoming their sinful relationships. For the sphere of human interrelationships is left entirely in human hands to create death-dealing or life-giving social structures. Here human beings cannot and should not plead that they are incapable of relating to their fellows in just and humane ways because it is within their power and ability to correct the destructive social structures that threaten to destroy and undermine their corporate life. By focusing on the area of human interrelationships, Black Theology will be making a substantial theological contribution to the Church at large by reminding all Christians that the central focus of the biblical message is that human beings should live and promote healthy relationships among themselves, and ultimately between human beings and their Creator.

By focusing on the centrality of these relationships, Black Theology would be enabling the Church to make necessary links between right believing and right doing, between faith and ethics — none of which can stand on its own without the other. In the past the Church was concerned that people should have the right belief, a correct dogma, regardless of whether what Christians do matched up to their verbal professions. Correcting this view, Black Theology should insist that the right belief (orthodoxy) and the right doing (orthopraxis) belong together; both are equally important tests of authenticity and integrity of the gospel. The emphasis on both aspects can be made only when Christians take seriously what they do to and with one another in society as the measure of their faith in God the Saviour. Put somewhat differently, the emphasis on the right belief and right doing (action) enables the Church to link once again human relationships between God and human beings and between human beings themselves. As theology makes this crucial link between the vertical and horizontal relationships, the Church will be calling Christians to account for what they do as people who try to live according to God's holy and loving will. In consequence, when people claim that they believe in God, it becomes necessary for them to demonstrate the authenticity of their faith through the way they live with their fellows in society. This testing of genuine faith by right actions has become necessary in both South Africa and North America.[9] For if people who claim that they are Christians were to live according to what they profess on Sunday, the so-called racial problems and their concomitant socio-political and economic oppression of one racial group by another would been effectively confronted and overcome. Therefore, the task and future relevance of Black Theology remain one of calling and challenging Christians to match their words by deeds in their relationships with their racially different neighbours in the light of what the gospel teaches them every Sunday. For it is as Christians do this that love, peace, justice, reconciliation and fellowship proclaimed and promised in the gospel will become realised and made more present in our conflict-ridden world.

FOOTNOTES:

1. Victorio, Araya, *God of the Poor,* Maryknoll: Orbis, 1987, pp.27-27; Jack, Nelson-Pallmeyer, *The politics of Compassion,* Maryknoll: Orbis, 1986, p.19
2. Qouted by Carter Lindberg, 'Through a Glass Darkly: A History of the Church's Vision on the Poor and Poverty' in *The Ecumenical Review* Vol.33, 1981, p.37.
3. Simon S Maimela, *Proclaim Freedom to my People,* Skotaville Publishers, Braamfontein: 1987, pp. 69-70; Araya, Victorio, *God of the Poor,* Maryknoll: Orbis, 1987, p.27
4. Mt 22:36-40; Mk 12:28-31
5. Dt 6:5, 10:12, Lv 19:11-18
6. John Driver, *Understanding the Atonement,* Scottdale, Pen.: Herald Press, 1986, p.30. Cf Mays, Benjamin, *Seeking to be Christian in Race Relations*, New York: Friendship Press, 1964, p.35.
7. Allan Boesak, *Farewell to Innocence*, Maryknoll: Orbis, 1977, p.152
8. I Jn 3:17-18; 4:12, 20-21
9. Jas 2:14-26

www.ingramcontent.com/pod-product-compliance
Lightning Source LLC
Chambersburg PA
CBHW051931160426
43198CB00012B/2101